THE FUTURE OF
VIDEO PLATFORMS

AI

STEM SCHOOL

The Future of Video Platforms

AI, Streaming and the Next Digital Revolution

By

STEM School

This Page Left Intentionally Blank

Contents

Chapter 1

Introduction to Video Platforms

The rise of video platforms has transformed the way people engage with content, communicate with one another, and access information. From the early days of television broadcasting to the modern era of on-demand streaming, video has established itself as one of the most influential mediums in human history. This chapter explores the evolution of video platforms, their impact on various sectors such as entertainment, education, and communication, and the emerging trends that are shaping the future of video technology, including live streaming, 4K resolution, and virtual reality.

Evolution of Video Platforms

The journey of video platforms began with the invention of television in the early 20th century. Television broadcasting allowed people to consume video content passively, with centralized networks delivering content on fixed schedules. The shift from black-and-white to color broadcasting in the mid-20th century marked a significant technological advancement, increasing viewer engagement and expanding the range of creative possibilities for producers and broadcasters.

The introduction of home video recording devices, such as the VHS (Video Home System) in the 1970s and 1980s, allowed viewers to record, store, and replay video content at their convenience. This marked the beginning of personalized media consumption, as viewers gained greater control over how and when they watched content. The rise of cable television in the 1980s and 1990s further expanded content availability, providing specialized channels dedicated to specific genres such as news, sports, music, and movies.

The internet era in the late 1990s and early 2000s led to the next major shift in video consumption. Platforms such as YouTube (founded in 2005) revolutionized the video landscape by enabling user-generated content and democratizing video publishing. Suddenly, anyone with a camera and an internet connection could become a content creator, reaching global audiences with minimal production costs. This new model of content distribution bypassed traditional gatekeepers, allowing for greater creative freedom and diversity in content.

Subscription-based streaming services such as Netflix, Hulu, and Amazon Prime emerged in the late 2000s and early 2010s, introducing the concept of on-demand content. Unlike traditional cable services, which required viewers to tune in at specific times, streaming platforms allowed users to access vast libraries of content at any time. This flexibility appealed to modern audiences, leading to the rapid decline of traditional cable television and the rise of "cord-cutting" — the practice of canceling cable subscriptions in favor of internet-based streaming.

Impact of Video Platforms

The rise of video platforms has had a profound impact on multiple aspects of society, particularly in the fields of entertainment, education, and communication.

In the **entertainment industry**, video platforms have transformed the way content is produced and consumed. Major film studios and television networks now compete with independent creators on platforms like YouTube, TikTok, and Twitch. Streaming services like Netflix and Disney+ have invested heavily in producing original content, challenging the dominance of traditional studios. The availability of on-demand content has also changed viewer habits, leading to "binge-watching" — the practice of watching multiple episodes of a series in one sitting.

The table below summarizes the shift in entertainment consumption patterns before and after the rise of streaming platforms

Aspect	Pre-Streaming Era	Streaming Era
Content Availability	Fixed broadcast schedules	On-demand access to content

Aspect	Pre-Streaming Era	Streaming Era
Viewer Control	Limited to broadcast times	Full control over viewing times
Content Creation	Dominated by major studios	Accessible to independent creators
Content Variety	Limited by broadcasting constraints	Virtually unlimited variety

In the field of **education**, video platforms have facilitated new methods of learning and knowledge sharing. Platforms like YouTube, Coursera, and Udemy allow educators to create and distribute instructional content to a global audience. Unlike traditional classroom settings, online video courses provide flexibility for students to learn at their own pace. Live streaming of lectures and interactive sessions has further enhanced the learning experience by allowing real-time interaction between instructors and students.

Educational institutions have also adapted to this shift by incorporating video-based learning into their curricula. Recorded lectures, instructional videos, and virtual classrooms have become integral components of modern education. The ability to pause, rewind, and review content has improved knowledge retention and allowed students to revisit complex concepts at their convenience.

The table below compares traditional learning methods with video-based education

Aspect	Traditional Learning	Video-Based Learning
Accessibility	Limited to classroom settings	Global access via internet
Flexibility	Fixed schedules	Self-paced learning
Interactivity	Limited to in-person sessions	Live streaming and interactive content
Retention	Dependent on real-time understanding	Ability to replay and review content

In the realm of **communication**, video platforms have changed how people connect with one another. Video calls, live streams, and social media video posts have become primary modes of interaction, especially with the rise of remote work and virtual events. Platforms like Zoom, Microsoft Teams, and Google Meet have enabled remote collaboration, allowing businesses to maintain productivity without the need for physical presence.

Social media platforms have also integrated video content into their ecosystems, with short-form videos becoming a dominant format. TikTok, Instagram Reels, and YouTube Shorts have capitalized on the popularity of quick, engaging content, influencing trends and shaping popular culture. The ability to broadcast live content has given rise to influencer culture, where individuals build massive followings and monetize their content through brand partnerships and advertisements.

Emerging Trends in Video Platforms

The video industry continues to evolve, driven by technological advancements and shifting user preferences. Three key trends are currently shaping the future of video platforms **live streaming**, **4K resolution**, and **virtual reality**.

Live Streaming has become a central feature of modern video platforms. Unlike pre-recorded content, live streams allow creators to interact with their audience in real time. Platforms like Twitch and YouTube Live have established dedicated communities around live content, ranging from gaming sessions and music performances to live Q&A sessions and product launches. The ability to receive immediate feedback from viewers has created a more interactive and engaging experience for both creators and audiences.

4K Resolution represents a significant leap in video quality, offering four times the pixel count of 1080p

HD content. Streaming platforms such as Netflix and Disney+ now offer a growing library of 4K content, enabling viewers to experience sharper images, richer colors, and greater detail. However, the higher data requirements for 4K streaming pose challenges for internet infrastructure, especially in regions with limited bandwidth.

The rise of **virtual reality (VR)** is redefining the boundaries of video content. VR platforms such as Oculus TV and YouTube VR allow users to immerse themselves in 360-degree video experiences. Unlike traditional flat-screen viewing, VR places the viewer inside the content, creating a more immersive and interactive experience. This technology has applications in entertainment, education, and training. For example, VR-based training simulations allow professionals to practice complex procedures in a controlled virtual environment, improving learning outcomes and reducing training costs.

The following table summarizes the key emerging trends in video platforms

Trend	Description	Impact
Live Streaming	Real-time video interaction	Greater audience engagement and creator feedback
4K	Higher pixel	Enhanced viewing

Trend	Description	Impact
Resolution	density and image quality	experience but higher data consumption
Virtual Reality	Immersive 360-degree video content	Interactive and lifelike viewing experience

The evolution of video platforms from traditional broadcasting to on-demand streaming and live content has fundamentally changed how people consume and engage with video. The rise of independent creators, the shift to personalized content consumption, and the integration of high-quality formats such as 4K and VR have made video platforms a dominant force in modern society. The impact of video platforms extends beyond entertainment, shaping how people learn, communicate, and work. As technology continues to evolve, the boundaries of video content creation and consumption will continue to expand, presenting new opportunities and challenges for creators and audiences alike.

Chapter 2

Core Technologies behind Video Platforms

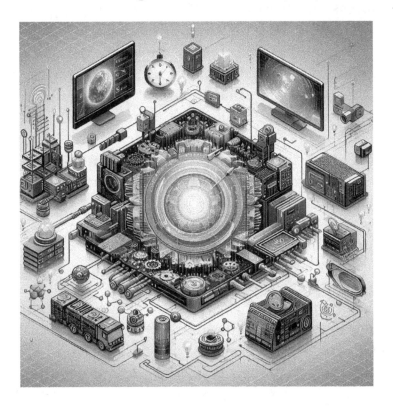

The success of modern video platforms is rooted in a complex and sophisticated technological infrastructure that enables seamless video delivery to millions of users worldwide. The ability to stream high-quality video content across different devices and network conditions requires a combination of advanced video compression algorithms, efficient streaming protocols, and robust Content Delivery Networks (CDNs). This chapter explores the core technologies that form the backbone of video platforms, including video compression algorithms such as H.264 and HEVC, streaming protocols like HLS and DASH, and the critical role of CDNs in reducing latency and improving streaming performance. Understanding these technologies is essential for building and maintaining a reliable and scalable video platform.

Video Compression Algorithms

Video compression algorithms are essential for reducing the size of video files without compromising their quality. Raw video data is incredibly large and would require enormous bandwidth and storage capacity if transmitted or stored without compression. For example, a single minute of uncompressed 1080p video at 30 frames per second (fps) would require several gigabytes of storage. Compression reduces the data size by removing redundant information and using predictive coding techniques while maintaining acceptable visual quality. The two most widely used video compression standards are **H.264 (Advanced Video Coding, AVC)** and **HEVC (High-Efficiency Video Coding, H.265)**.

H.264 (AVC) was introduced in 2003 and became the dominant video compression standard due to its balance between compression efficiency and computational complexity. H.264 uses a combination of intra-frame and inter-frame compression. Intra-frame compression reduces redundancy within a single frame by analyzing patterns and similarities, while inter-frame compression reduces redundancy across frames by identifying and encoding motion vectors.

H.264 employs several key techniques, including

Macroblocks and Transform Coding – Each video frame is divided into 16x16-pixel macroblocks. The data within each macroblock is transformed using the Discrete Cosine Transform (DCT) to convert spatial information into frequency components, which can then be compressed more efficiently.

Motion Compensation – When encoding a video sequence, H.264 predicts future frames based on motion vectors extracted from previous frames. Instead of encoding the entire frame, only the difference between the predicted frame and the actual frame is encoded, reducing data size.

Entropy Coding – H.264 uses Context-Adaptive Binary Arithmetic Coding (CABAC) or Context-Adaptive Variable-Length Coding (CAVLC) to encode the compressed data efficiently.

While H.264 remains widely used, its limitations in handling higher resolutions and frame rates have led to the development of more advanced standards such as **HEVC (H.265)**.

HEVC (H.265) was introduced in 2013 to address the increasing demand for high-resolution video content, including 4K and 8K formats. HEVC achieves approximately **50% better compression efficiency** than H.264 at the same visual quality. This means that HEVC requires only half the bandwidth to deliver the same quality video stream as H.264.

HEVC improves upon H.264 by introducing several advanced techniques

Coding Tree Units (CTUs) – Instead of using fixed-size macroblocks, HEVC divides frames into Coding Tree Units (CTUs) that can vary in size from 8x8 to 64x64 pixels. Larger CTUs improve compression efficiency by reducing the number of blocks needed to represent an image.

Improved Motion Compensation – HEVC allows for more complex motion prediction using finer motion vectors and greater prediction accuracy.

Advanced Transform Coding – HEVC uses both DCT and Discrete Sine Transform (DST) to achieve higher compression efficiency for complex patterns.

Parallel Processing – HEVC is designed for efficient parallel processing, making it more suitable for modern multi-core processors and hardware-based encoding solutions.

The table below compares H.264 and HEVC compression standards

Feature	H.264 (AVC)	HEVC (H.265)
Compression Efficiency	Moderate	High (50% better than H.264)
Resolution Support	Up to 4K	Up to 8K
Motion Prediction	Simple	Complex and more accurate
Coding Unit Size	Fixed (16x16)	Flexible (8x8 to 64x64)
Complexity	Lower	Higher (requires more processing power)

Streaming Protocols

Streaming protocols define how video data is transmitted over the internet. Unlike file downloads, which require the entire file to be downloaded before viewing, streaming protocols allow video content to be delivered in small chunks and played in real-time as the data arrives. This enables instant playback, adaptive quality adjustment, and real-time error correction.

The two most widely used streaming protocols are **HLS (HTTP Live Streaming)** and **DASH (Dynamic Adaptive Streaming over HTTP)**.

HLS (HTTP Live Streaming) was developed by Apple and introduced in 2009. HLS divides video content into small chunks (usually 2 to 10 seconds) and stores them as separate HTTP files. The video player downloads and buffers these chunks while simultaneously playing them.

HLS supports **adaptive bitrate streaming**, which allows the player to adjust the quality of the video stream based on the viewer's internet connection. If the bandwidth drops, the player automatically switches to a lower-resolution stream to prevent buffering. If the bandwidth improves, the player increases the quality.

DASH (Dynamic Adaptive Streaming over HTTP) is an open standard introduced in 2012 by the MPEG group. DASH works similarly to HLS but supports a wider range of encoding formats and platforms. DASH also uses adaptive bitrate streaming, allowing the player to switch between different quality levels in real-time.

The table below compares HLS and DASH

Feature	HLS	DASH
Developer	Apple	MPEG Group
Adaptive Bitrate	Yes	Yes
Codec Support	H.264, HEVC	H.264, HEVC, VP9, AV1
Platform Compatibility	iOS, macOS, Android, Windows	Cross-platform
Latency	Moderate	Low (with low-latency mode)

Content Delivery Networks (CDNs)

Content Delivery Networks (CDNs) are crucial for ensuring fast and reliable video delivery to a global audience. A CDN consists of a network of geographically distributed servers that cache copies of video content and deliver them to viewers from the nearest server.

When a user requests to play a video, the request is routed to the nearest CDN server, reducing latency and improving load times. CDNs also help distribute network traffic, preventing server overload and ensuring consistent performance during high-traffic events, such as live broadcasts.

Key advantages of CDNs for video streaming include

Reduced Latency – By serving content from a local server, CDNs minimize the physical distance that data must travel, reducing latency.

Load Balancing – CDNs distribute requests across multiple servers, preventing any single server from becoming overloaded.

Scalability – CDNs allow video platforms to handle millions of concurrent viewers without compromising performance.

Redundancy and Failover – CDNs replicate content across multiple servers, ensuring that if one server fails, another can take over without service interruption.

The diagram below illustrates how a CDN functions in a video streaming context

User Request→Nearest CDN Server→Cached Video Del ivery\text{User Request} \rightarrow \text{Nearest CDN Server} \rightarrow \text{Cached Video Delivery}User Request→Nearest CDN Server→Cached Video Delivery

The technical infrastructure behind modern video platforms relies on a combination of compression algorithms, streaming protocols, and CDNs. Compression algorithms such as H.264 and HEVC reduce the size of video files without sacrificing quality, making them suitable for streaming over limited bandwidth connections. Streaming protocols like HLS and DASH enable real-time playback and adaptive quality adjustments, ensuring a smooth viewing experience under varying network conditions. CDNs provide the scalability and reliability necessary to deliver video content to millions of viewers worldwide with minimal latency and buffering. Mastering these core technologies is essential for building a competitive and high-performing video platform in the modern digital landscape.

Chapter 3

Building a Video Platform Architecture

Building a video platform architecture requires a comprehensive and well-thought-out design that addresses the challenges of storing, processing, delivering, and displaying video content efficiently and reliably. A video platform must be capable of handling large volumes of data, supporting high-quality video playback, and providing a seamless user experience across multiple devices and network conditions. This involves integrating server-side video storage and processing with a responsive and scalable front-end application. A properly designed video platform architecture must account for scalability, load balancing, fault tolerance, and content security to ensure consistent performance and high availability. This chapter explores the step-by-step process of designing the architecture of a video platform, providing insights into the technical requirements and best practices for building a scalable and reliable solution.

Overview of Video Platform Architecture

A video platform architecture consists of several interconnected components that work together to deliver video content from the server to the end-user device. These components include

- **Video Ingestion and Storage** The process of uploading and storing raw video files in a centralized repository.
- **Video Processing** Encoding, transcoding, and compressing raw video files into multiple formats and resolutions for efficient delivery.
- **Content Delivery** Distribution of processed video files to end users using streaming protocols and Content Delivery Networks (CDNs).
- **User Interface** The front-end application that enables users to search, browse, and stream video content.
- **Analytics and Monitoring** Tracking user engagement, stream quality, and performance metrics to improve user experience and platform reliability.

The diagram below illustrates the overall architecture of a video platform

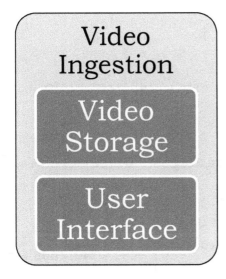 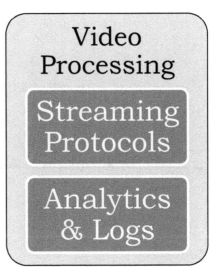

Video Ingestion and Storage

The first step in building a video platform is to create a reliable and scalable video ingestion and storage system. When a user uploads a video, the platform must store the file in a secure and accessible repository. This involves handling large file sizes, managing metadata, and ensuring data integrity.

File Storage Solutions

Video files can be stored using different storage architectures, including object storage, block storage, and file storage. Object storage is the most common solution for video platforms due to its scalability and cost efficiency. Services like Amazon S3, Google Cloud Storage, and Azure Blob Storage provide highly durable and available object storage solutions for video content.

The table below compares different storage architectures

Storage Type	Description	Advantages	Disadvantages
Object Storage	Data stored as objects with metadata and unique identifiers	Highly scalable, cost-effective, supports large files	Higher latency for small files
Block Storage	Data stored in fixed-size blocks, similar to a hard drive	Fast data retrieval, suitable for structured data	Limited scalability, higher cost
File Storage	Data stored in hierarchical files and folders	Simple to manage, supports file-based access	Difficult to scale for large volumes

Metadata Management

Every uploaded video should be accompanied by metadata that includes the file name, size, duration, resolution, codec, and author information. Metadata enables efficient content indexing, search, and retrieval. The metadata can be stored in a relational database like MySQL or a NoSQL database like MongoDB for fast access and querying.

Video Processing

Once a video file is stored, it must be processed before it can be streamed to end users. Processing includes encoding, transcoding, and compression.

Encoding converts the raw video file into a digital format suitable for transmission and playback. Common encoding formats include H.264, HEVC (H.265), and VP9.

Transcoding creates multiple versions of the same video at different resolutions and bitrates. This allows the platform to support adaptive bitrate streaming, where the video quality can be adjusted dynamically based on the viewer's network conditions.

Compression reduces the size of video files while maintaining visual quality. Modern compression algorithms like H.264 and HEVC allow for high-quality video delivery with minimal bandwidth consumption.

The table below outlines the different encoding formats and their characteristics

Encoding Format	Compression Efficiency	Supported Resolutions	Common Use Cases
H.264 (AVC)	Moderate	Up to 4K	Standard streaming, live video
HEVC (H.265)	High (50% better than H.264)	Up to 8K	High-resolution streaming, 4K UHD
VP9	High	Up to 4K	Web streaming, YouTube
AV1	Very High	Up to 8K	Next-gen video platforms

Content Delivery and Streaming

Delivering video content efficiently requires the use of adaptive streaming protocols such as **HLS (HTTP Live Streaming)** and **DASH (Dynamic Adaptive Streaming over HTTP)**. These protocols divide video content into small chunks that are dynamically delivered based on network conditions.

To minimize latency and buffering, video platforms use Content Delivery Networks (CDNs). CDNs cache video content at multiple server locations worldwide, reducing the distance between the user and the video file. This ensures faster load times and more consistent playback quality. Load balancing is also critical for managing incoming traffic. A load balancer distributes incoming user requests across multiple servers to prevent overloading and maximize server efficiency.

Front-End User Interface

The front-end user interface (UI) is the point of interaction between the user and the video platform. A well-designed UI should offer a seamless browsing and viewing experience.

The UI should include features like

- Search and filtering capabilities to help users find relevant content quickly.
- Watchlists and recommendations based on user behavior.
- Multi-device support, including web browsers, mobile apps, smart TVs, and game consoles.
- Playback controls, including play, pause, skip, and volume adjustment.

User sessions should be managed using secure authentication protocols like OAuth 2.0 to ensure user privacy and data security.

Analytics and Monitoring

Analytics play a crucial role in optimizing platform performance and improving user engagement. Real-time monitoring of video streaming performance, buffer rates, and user engagement helps in identifying issues and improving the user experience.

Key performance metrics include

- Video start time (time taken to load the video).
- Buffering ratio (percentage of playback time spent buffering).
- Average bitrate (average quality of streamed video).
- User session length and retention rates.

The collected data can be visualized using analytical dashboards to track user behavior and platform performance.

Designing a scalable and reliable video platform architecture requires a deep understanding of video ingestion, storage, processing, delivery, and user interaction. Effective video storage and encoding solutions ensure that video files are delivered efficiently, while adaptive streaming protocols and CDNs guarantee consistent playback quality under varying network conditions. A responsive and feature-rich front-end interface enhances user experience, while real-time analytics and monitoring provide insights into platform performance and user engagement. By following best practices for scalability, load balancing, and fault tolerance, developers can create a robust video platform capable of handling high traffic volumes and delivering high-quality content to a global audience.

Chapter 4

Video Encoding and Compression

Video encoding and compression are two of the most critical processes in the video production and delivery pipeline. Encoding refers to the process of converting raw video files into a digital format suitable for playback, storage, and transmission, while compression reduces the file size of encoded videos without significantly compromising visual quality. Efficient encoding and compression are essential for ensuring that video platforms can deliver high-quality video content over a wide range of network conditions and devices while minimizing bandwidth consumption and storage requirements.

Encoding and compression directly impact the overall user experience by determining the visual quality of the video, the time required to load and buffer content, and the compatibility of the video with different devices and playback platforms. Achieving an optimal balance between compression efficiency and video quality requires an in-depth understanding of encoding techniques, compression algorithms, and the trade-offs involved in different encoding settings. This chapter explores the technical foundations of video encoding and compression, the tools and software available for video encoding, and the practical applications of different encoding settings.

Fundamentals of Video Encoding

Video encoding involves the conversion of raw video data into a structured format that can be efficiently stored and transmitted. Raw video files are typically large and uncompressed, making them unsuitable for direct streaming or storage. Encoding reduces the size of video files by removing redundant and non-essential data while preserving the visual and auditory quality of the content.

Raw video data consists of a sequence of images (frames) displayed at a specific frame rate. Each frame is composed of millions of pixels, each represented by color and brightness values. Encoding reduces the size of this data by using mathematical algorithms to remove redundant information and represent the data more efficiently.

Video encoding is performed using codecs (compressor-decompressor). A codec is an algorithm that encodes raw video into a compressed format and decodes the compressed video during playback. There are two main types of encoding

Lossy Encoding Lossy encoding reduces file size by permanently discarding some visual information. This results in a smaller file size at the cost of reduced image quality. Common lossy encoding codecs include H.264, HEVC, and VP9.

Lossless Encoding   Lossless encoding reduces file size without sacrificing any visual data. The file can be decompressed back to its original form without any quality loss. However, lossless encoding results in larger file sizes, making it less practical for streaming. Common lossless codecs include FFV1 and HuffYUV.

The table below outlines the differences between lossy and lossless encoding

Encoding Type	File Size Reduction	Quality	Common Use Cases
Lossy Encoding	High	Some quality loss	Streaming, online delivery, social media
Lossless Encoding	Moderate to Low	No quality loss	Archiving, post-production editing

Common Video Codecs

Different video codecs are designed to achieve different balances between compression efficiency, quality, and compatibility. The most commonly used video codecs are H.264 (AVC), H.265 (HEVC), VP9, and AV1.

H.264 (AVC)

H.264, also known as Advanced Video Coding (AVC), is one of the most widely used codecs in video platforms. It offers a good balance between compression efficiency and quality, making it suitable for streaming and live broadcasting. H.264 supports resolutions up to 4K and provides low latency, making it ideal for real-time video delivery.

H.265 (HEVC)

H.265, or High-Efficiency Video Coding (HEVC), is the successor to H.264. It offers approximately 50% better compression efficiency than H.264 while maintaining the same quality. This allows video platforms to deliver higher-quality content at lower bitrates. HEVC is well-suited for 4K and 8K streaming but requires more processing power for encoding and decoding.

VP9

VP9 is an open-source codec developed by Google. It provides similar compression efficiency to HEVC but does not require licensing fees. VP9 is widely used by platforms like YouTube and is optimized for web-based streaming.

AV1

AV1 is the most recent and advanced video codec, offering 30% better compression efficiency than VP9 and HEVC. It is supported by major technology companies, including Google, Apple, and Netflix. AV1 is designed for high-quality streaming at reduced bitrates but requires significant computational resources for encoding.

The table below compares the most common video codecs

Codec	Compression Efficiency	Quality	Processing Requirements	Common Use Cases
H.264 (AVC)	Moderate	Good	Low	Live streaming, standard video delivery
H.265 (HEVC)	High (50% better than H.264)	Excellent	High	4K and 8K streaming
VP9	High (similar to HEVC)	Excellent	Moderate	Web-based streaming (YouTube)
AV1	Very High (30% better than HEVC)	Excellent	Very High	Next-gen streaming, low-bandwidth

Codec	Compression Efficiency	Quality	Processing Requirements	Common Use Cases
				networks

Video Compression Techniques

Video compression reduces file size by removing redundant and non-essential information. There are three primary types of compression used in video encoding

Intra-Frame Compression

Intra-frame compression reduces file size by compressing each frame independently. It removes redundant pixel data within each frame using techniques like Discrete Cosine Transform (DCT) and Huffman coding. This type of compression provides high-quality results but requires more storage.

Inter-Frame Compression

Inter-frame compression reduces file size by compressing differences between consecutive frames rather than compressing each frame independently. It uses three types of frames

- **I-Frames (Intra-coded frames)** Self-contained frames that do not depend on other frames.
- **P-Frames (Predicted frames)** Frames that store only the changes relative to the previous frame.
- **B-Frames (Bidirectional frames)** Frames that store changes relative to both previous and future frames.

Adaptive Bitrate Streaming (ABR)

Adaptive bitrate streaming dynamically adjusts the video quality based on the user's network conditions and device capabilities. ABR requires encoding the video in multiple bitrates and resolutions. The streaming server automatically switches between different streams based on network speed and device capacity.

The diagram below illustrates inter-frame compression

Practical Trade-Offs in Encoding Settings

Encoding settings affect the trade-off between encoding speed, file size, and quality. Higher compression efficiency reduces file size but increases encoding time and computational load.

Bitrate Control

Bitrate determines the amount of data processed per second of video playback.

Constant Bitrate (CBR) Maintains a fixed bitrate throughout the video.

Variable Bitrate (VBR) Adjusts the bitrate dynamically based on content complexity.

Frame Rate

Higher frame rates improve motion smoothness but increase file size and processing requirements.

24 fps – Standard for cinematic videos

30 fps – Standard for TV broadcasts

60 fps – High frame rate for smooth action sequences and sports

Resolution

Higher resolutions provide greater visual detail but increase file size and bandwidth requirements.

1080p (Full HD) – Standard for high-definition streaming

4K (UHD) – Requires high bandwidth, suitable for premium content

8K (UHD-2) – High-resolution content for large screens

The table below summarizes the trade-offs between encoding settings

Setting	Effect on Quality	Effect on File Size	Effect on Encoding Speed
High Bitrate	High	Large	Slow
Low Bitrate	Low	Small	Fast
High Frame Rate	Smooth	Large	Slow
Low Frame Rate	Choppy	Small	Fast

Efficient video encoding and compression are essential for delivering high-quality video content while minimizing storage and bandwidth requirements. Choosing the right codec and encoding settings depends on the target platform, network conditions, and user expectations. Modern codecs like H.265 and AV1 offer excellent compression efficiency, but they require higher processing power for encoding and decoding. Adaptive bitrate streaming ensures that users receive the best possible quality under varying network conditions, while intra-frame and inter-frame compression techniques allow for efficient data reduction without significant loss of quality.

Chapter 5

Live Streaming and Real-Time Video Delivery

Live streaming and real-time video delivery have become central to the modern digital ecosystem. With the rise of social media platforms, online gaming, virtual events, and live broadcasts, the demand for efficient and scalable live streaming solutions has increased significantly. Unlike traditional video delivery, which involves pre-recorded content that is encoded, stored, and streamed on demand, live streaming involves capturing, encoding, transmitting, and delivering video content in real-time with minimal delay. This introduces a unique set of challenges, including low latency, variable network conditions, and consistent video quality across different devices and platforms.

Real-time video delivery requires a highly optimized pipeline that can handle the dynamic nature of live content. A well-designed live streaming platform must minimize latency to create a seamless user experience while adapting to changes in network bandwidth and device capabilities. Adaptive bitrate streaming, low-latency protocols, and real-time communication technologies are essential for ensuring smooth and reliable live video delivery. This chapter explores the technical foundations of live streaming and real-time video delivery, the protocols used for transmission, and the architectural considerations involved in building a scalable streaming platform.

Fundamentals of Live Streaming

Live streaming involves capturing video content from a source, encoding it into a suitable format, transmitting it over a network, and delivering it to viewers in real-time. The primary goal of live streaming is to minimize the time gap between capturing and playback while maintaining acceptable video quality. Unlike on-demand video streaming, which allows buffering and preloading to manage network variability, live streaming must handle network fluctuations and processing delays dynamically.

The live streaming workflow consists of several key stages

Capture The video signal is captured using a camera or other input device. The raw video feed is sent to the encoding stage.

Encoding The captured video feed is compressed and encoded using a codec such as H.264 or H.265. Encoding reduces the file size and ensures compatibility with various streaming platforms.

Packaging The encoded video stream is packaged into a suitable format for transmission, such as MPEG-DASH, HLS, or WebRTC.

Transmission The packaged stream is transmitted over the internet using a protocol like RTMP (Real-Time

Messaging Protocol) or WebRTC (Web Real-Time Communication).

Decoding and Playback The stream is decoded and played back by the viewer's device. Adaptive bitrate streaming (ABR) allows the player to adjust the video quality based on network conditions and device capabilities.

Challenges of Live Streaming

Live streaming presents several technical challenges that distinguish it from on-demand video delivery.

Latency

Latency refers to the time delay between the capture of the video and its display on the viewer's screen. High latency can disrupt real-time interaction and reduce the quality of experience, especially for live events such as sports broadcasts and online gaming. Traditional live streaming platforms using HTTP-based protocols like HLS (HTTP Live Streaming) and MPEG-DASH typically have latencies ranging from 10 to 30 seconds, which is unacceptable for real-time applications.

Network Variability

Live streaming over the internet is subject to fluctuating network bandwidth and packet loss.

Network congestion can cause video stuttering, buffering, and quality degradation. Adaptive bitrate streaming (ABR) addresses this challenge by dynamically adjusting the video quality based on available bandwidth.

Device Compatibility

Viewers use a wide range of devices to access live streams, including smartphones, smart TVs, gaming consoles, and computers. A live streaming platform must support multiple codecs and transmission protocols to ensure compatibility with different hardware and operating systems.

Scalability

Large-scale live streaming requires a highly scalable infrastructure capable of handling thousands or even millions of simultaneous viewers. Content delivery networks (CDNs) are used to distribute live streams globally and reduce latency by serving content from servers located close to viewers.

Low-Latency Streaming Protocols

Several streaming protocols have been developed to minimize latency and improve the real-time performance of live video delivery. The choice of protocol impacts the balance between latency, scalability, and device compatibility.

WebRTC (Web Real-Time Communication)

WebRTC is a peer-to-peer communication protocol designed for low-latency real-time communication. It enables direct transmission of video, audio, and data between browsers and devices without the need for additional plugins or software. WebRTC achieves latency as low as 100 milliseconds, making it ideal for real-time interactive applications such as video conferencing and live auctions.

WebRTC uses UDP (User Datagram Protocol) instead of TCP (Transmission Control Protocol) for faster data transmission. UDP does not require packet acknowledgment, which reduces latency but can lead to packet loss under poor network conditions. WebRTC includes mechanisms for error correction and packet recovery to address this issue.

RTMP (Real-Time Messaging Protocol)

RTMP is a widely used protocol for live video transmission developed by Adobe. It is based on TCP and provides reliable data transmission with low latency. RTMP is commonly used for ingesting video streams from encoders to streaming servers. However, it is not natively supported by most browsers, which limits its use for end-to-end delivery.

RTMP provides latency between 1 to 3 seconds, making it suitable for live streaming events and interactive broadcasts. Many live streaming platforms use RTMP for video ingestion and convert the stream into HLS or MPEG-DASH for wider compatibility.

HLS (HTTP Live Streaming)

HLS is an HTTP-based streaming protocol developed by Apple. It divides video streams into small segments (typically 2 to 10 seconds) and delivers them over standard HTTP connections. HLS provides excellent compatibility with browsers, mobile devices, and smart TVs.

HLS supports adaptive bitrate streaming, allowing the player to adjust the video quality based on network conditions. However, HLS typically has higher latency (10 to 30 seconds) due to segment buffering and HTTP-based delivery. Low-latency HLS (LL-HLS) has been introduced to reduce latency to 2 to 5 seconds by shortening segment duration and enabling partial segment delivery.

Adaptive Bitrate Streaming (ABR)

Adaptive bitrate streaming (ABR) is a key technology for improving the quality of experience in live streaming. ABR allows the video player to switch between different video quality levels based on available bandwidth and network conditions.

In ABR, the encoder generates multiple video streams at different bitrates and resolutions. The video player monitors network performance and automatically switches to the most suitable stream.

Bitrate	Resolution	Frame Rate	Quality	Bandwidth Requirement
1 Mbps	480p	30 fps	Medium	Low
3 Mbps	720p	30 fps	High	Moderate
5 Mbps	1080p	60 fps	Very High	High
15 Mbps	4K	60 fps	Ultra High	Very High

ABR improves the viewing experience by minimizing buffering and maintaining smooth playback even under variable network conditions. It also reduces the load on the streaming server by distributing the traffic across multiple quality levels.

Architecture of a Live Streaming Platform

A typical live streaming platform consists of several components that work together to capture, encode, transmit, and deliver video streams.

Encoder Compresses and formats the video stream using a codec like H.264 or H.265. **Ingest Server** Receives the encoded video stream and forwards it to the streaming server. **Streaming Server** Distributes the video stream to a CDN (Content Delivery Network) for global delivery. **CDN** Delivers the video stream to viewers based on their geographic location. **Player** Decodes and plays the video stream on the viewer's device.

The diagram below illustrates a typical live streaming architecture

1 • Encoder

2 • Ingest Server

3 • Streaming Server

The use of CDNs allows live streaming platforms to handle large traffic volumes and minimize latency by serving content from the closest server to the viewer.

Live streaming and real-time video delivery require a carefully designed infrastructure to handle latency, network variability, and scalability. WebRTC and RTMP provide low-latency delivery for real-time communication, while HLS and MPEG-DASH offer broader compatibility at the cost of higher latency. Adaptive bitrate streaming enhances the viewing experience by dynamically adjusting video quality based on network performance. A well-architected live streaming platform leverages these technologies to deliver high-quality, low-latency video content to viewers worldwide.

Chapter 6

Video Storage and Content Management

Efficient video storage and content management are critical components of any video streaming or delivery platform. As the volume of video content increases, the challenges associated with storing, organizing, and managing large video libraries become more complex. The storage infrastructure must handle the high data rates and large file sizes associated with video files, while ensuring quick access, scalability, and redundancy to prevent data loss. Additionally, content management systems (CMS) play a crucial role in organizing video content, tagging it with metadata, and making it searchable and accessible to users. Effective content management improves the user experience by enabling fast content discovery, personalized recommendations, and efficient delivery across multiple platforms.

Modern video storage solutions leverage both cloud-based and on-premises infrastructure to provide a balance between scalability, cost-effectiveness, and performance. Cloud-based solutions offer virtually unlimited storage capacity, global distribution, and redundancy, while on-premises storage solutions provide greater control over data security, latency, and access speeds. Hybrid storage models that combine both cloud and local storage are increasingly common, allowing platforms to store frequently accessed content locally while offloading less critical content to the cloud.

This chapter explores the technical foundations of video storage and content management, examining the different storage architectures, the role of content management systems, and the techniques used for indexing and metadata tagging. It also provides practical insights into designing a scalable and efficient video storage infrastructure to support large-scale video delivery platforms.

Understanding Video Storage Requirements

Video files are significantly larger than other types of media due to their high data rates, frame rates, and resolution. A single 1080p video file encoded at 60 frames per second (fps) using the H.264 codec can require a bitrate of around 5 Mbps, which translates to approximately 2.25 GB per hour of video content. Higher resolutions such as 4K (3840 x 2160) or 8K (7680 x 4320) can increase the storage requirements by a factor of four to sixteen times, depending on the encoding and compression settings.

The table below provides an overview of typical storage requirements for different video formats and bitrates

Resolution	Frame Rate	Bitrate	Storage per Hour	Compression Codec
480p (SD)	30 fps	1 Mbps	450 MB	H.264

Resolution	Frame Rate	Bitrate	Storage per Hour	Compression Codec
720p (HD)	30 fps	3 Mbps	1.35 GB	H.264
1080p (Full HD)	60 fps	5 Mbps	2.25 GB	H.264
4K (Ultra HD)	60 fps	15 Mbps	6.75 GB	H.265
8K (Super HD)	60 fps	40 Mbps	18 GB	H.265

The high storage demands of video content require a carefully designed storage architecture that can accommodate large file sizes while supporting fast data retrieval and processing.

Types of Video Storage Solutions

Video storage solutions can be broadly classified into three main categories on-premises storage, cloud-based storage, and hybrid storage. Each type has advantages and trade-offs in terms of cost, scalability, security, and access speed.

On-Premises Storage

On-premises storage refers to storing video files on local servers or storage arrays physically located within the data center or organization. This type of storage provides high-speed access to video files, low latency, and full control over data security and management.

On-premises storage solutions typically use high-capacity hard disk drives (HDDs) or solid-state drives (SSDs) configured in a RAID (Redundant Array of Independent Disks) setup to provide fault tolerance and redundancy. Storage Area Networks (SANs) and Network Attached Storage (NAS) are commonly used for large-scale video storage.

A SAN is a dedicated high-speed network that connects multiple storage devices to a central server, allowing for fast data transfer and high availability. NAS, on the other hand, connects storage devices directly to the local network, enabling direct access to video files from multiple devices.

Storage Type	Speed	Scalability	Cost	Security	Use Case
HDD (RAID)	Moderate	Moderate	Low	High	Archive and

Storage Type	Speed	Scalability	Cost	Security	Use Case
					backup
SSD	High	Moderate	High	High	High-speed access and editing
SAN	Very High	High	High	High	Enterprise-scale video storage
NAS	Moderate	High	Moderate	Moderate	Small-to-medium businesses

The primary advantage of on-premises storage is that it provides low-latency access to video files and greater control over data security. However, it requires significant capital investment in hardware and maintenance, which may not be feasible for smaller platforms.

Cloud-Based Storage

Cloud-based storage involves storing video files on remote servers managed by cloud service providers such as Amazon Web Services (AWS), Google Cloud, and Microsoft Azure. Cloud storage offers virtually unlimited capacity, geographic redundancy, and automatic backups.

Cloud storage providers typically offer different storage tiers based on access frequency and latency requirements. Frequently accessed video files are stored in high-performance storage classes, while less frequently accessed files are moved to low-cost archival storage.

Cloud Storage Type	Access Speed	Cost	Use Case
Standard Storage	High	High	Frequently accessed content
Nearline Storage	Moderate	Moderate	Infrequently accessed content
Coldline Storage	Low	Low	Long-term archival
Archive Storage	Very Low	Very Low	Rarely accessed backup files

Cloud-based storage reduces the need for hardware investment and provides built-in scalability. However, it introduces higher latency due to network transmission and may incur significant costs for data transfer and retrieval.

Hybrid Storage

Hybrid storage combines on-premises and cloud-based storage to optimize cost, performance, and scalability. Frequently accessed or high-priority content is stored on local servers to provide low-latency access, while less frequently accessed content is offloaded to cloud storage.

A hybrid storage architecture uses a caching layer to automatically migrate video files between local and cloud storage based on access patterns and demand. This approach reduces costs while maintaining high performance for real-time video delivery.

Content Management Systems (CMS) for Video

A video content management system (CMS) is a software platform used to organize, store, retrieve, and distribute video content. A CMS provides a centralized interface for managing large video libraries, assigning metadata, and controlling user access.

Metadata Tagging

Metadata tagging involves assigning descriptive information to video files to make them searchable and discoverable. Metadata includes information such as title, description, duration, resolution, encoding format, frame rate, and content categories.

Metadata Type	Description	Example
Title	Name of the video	"Product Launch Event 2025"
Description	Summary of the content	"Highlights from the 2025 product launch event"
Duration	Length of the video	45 minutes
Format	Encoding and container format	H.264, MP4
Category	Content type	Event, Tutorial, Documentary

A well-tagged video library enables fast search and content discovery, improving the user experience and enabling personalized recommendations.

Video Indexing

Video indexing involves creating a searchable database of video content. Modern video CMS platforms use AI-based indexing to analyze video content, extract key information, and automatically generate metadata. Speech-to-text conversion, face recognition, and scene detection are commonly used for automated video indexing.

Designing a Scalable Video Storage Architecture

A scalable video storage architecture must balance the need for high-speed access, large storage capacity, and data redundancy. The ideal architecture involves a multi-tier storage model with a caching layer, a CDN for global delivery, and automated migration between storage tiers based on demand.

The diagram below illustrates a typical scalable video storage architecture

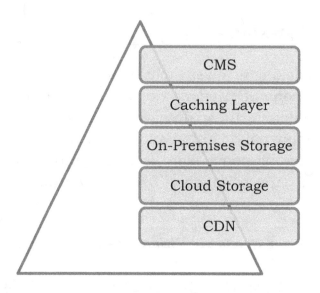

The CMS manages metadata and user access, while the caching layer improves access speed by storing frequently accessed content locally. Cloud storage ensures scalability, while the CDN reduces latency by serving content from edge servers close to the viewer.

Effective video storage and content management are critical for building scalable and high-performance video delivery platforms. A combination of on-premises and cloud-based storage provides a balance between cost and performance. Metadata tagging and automated video indexing improve content discoverability and user experience. A scalable architecture with a multi-tier storage model ensures fast access, redundancy, and global availability for large video libraries.

Chapter 7

Building a Video Player

A video player is the interface through which users engage with video content, making it one of the most critical components of any video delivery platform. A well-designed video player not only enables smooth playback of video content but also enhances user engagement through an intuitive and responsive interface. The development of a custom video player requires a deep understanding of video formats, encoding, streaming protocols, and device compatibility. Furthermore, the performance of the video player, including load times, buffering, and responsiveness, directly affects the user experience (UX) and retention rates.

Designing a custom video player involves several key challenges, including handling different video codecs and formats, ensuring playback across different devices and operating systems, supporting adaptive bitrate streaming to optimize performance under varying network conditions, and integrating user-friendly controls for playback, volume, and navigation. A custom video player must also support various accessibility features, including closed captions, subtitles, and audio descriptions, to provide an inclusive viewing experience.

Modern video players are integrated into both web-based and mobile applications, requiring developers to account for the differences in hardware capabilities, screen sizes, operating systems, and browser support. For web applications, HTML5 and JavaScript provide a solid foundation for building custom video players, while mobile applications typically rely on platform-specific frameworks such as Android's ExoPlayer or Apple's AVPlayer.

This chapter explores the technical foundations of building a custom video player, covering the key architectural components, supported video formats, streaming protocols, and techniques for performance optimization and cross-device compatibility. It also provides practical insights into enhancing the user experience through intuitive controls, customization options, and advanced playback features.

Architectural Components of a Video Player

A video player consists of several core components that work together to decode, buffer, and display video content in real time. The architecture of a video player includes the following key components

Media Source – The media source represents the input video file or stream, which can be stored locally or delivered through a content delivery network (CDN).

Decoder – The decoder processes the encoded video and audio data, converting it into raw frames that can be rendered on the screen.

Renderer – The renderer handles the presentation of decoded video frames and audio samples, synchronizing playback with the display.

Buffer – The buffer temporarily stores decoded frames and audio samples to smooth out playback and prevent interruptions due to network congestion.

User Interface (UI) – The UI includes playback controls, progress bars, volume controls, and settings that allow the user to interact with the video player.

Network Handler – The network handler manages data transmission between the media source and the player, handling network errors and reconnections.

This modular architecture ensures that different components can be upgraded or modified independently to improve performance and compatibility. The decoder and renderer are tightly integrated to minimize latency and ensure smooth playback, while the buffer acts as a shock absorber to prevent stuttering due to network issues.

Supported Video Formats and Codecs

A video player must support a wide range of video formats and codecs to ensure compatibility across different devices and platforms. Video files are typically encoded using codecs that compress the data to reduce file size while preserving video quality. The container format determines how the encoded video and audio streams are packaged together.

Common Video Codecs

The most widely used video codecs include

Codec	Description	Compression Efficiency	Supported Platforms
H.264 (AVC)	Most commonly used codec for video streaming	High	All major platforms and browsers
H.265 (HEVC)	Successor to H.264 with better compression efficiency	Very High	Supported on modern hardware and platforms
VP8	Open-source codec developed by Google	Moderate	Supported on most browsers except Safari
VP9	Successor to VP8 with higher efficiency	High	Supported on most modern browsers
AV1	Next-generation codec with improved	Very High	Supported on modern browsers and

Codec	Description	Compression Efficiency	Supported Platforms
	efficiency		hardware

Common Container Formats

Container formats define how video and audio streams are packaged together. The most widely used container formats include

Format	Description	Supported Codecs
MP4	Most widely supported container format	H.264, H.265, AAC
WebM	Open-source format designed for web streaming	VP8, VP9, Opus
MKV	Versatile format supporting multiple streams and subtitles	H.264, VP9, AAC
MOV	Apple's proprietary format for high-quality video	H.264, H.265, AAC

Compatibility with different container formats ensures that the video player can handle content from various sources and platforms.

Adaptive Bitrate Streaming (ABR)

Adaptive bitrate streaming (ABR) allows the video player to adjust the quality of the video stream in real time based on network conditions and device capabilities. ABR improves playback performance and reduces buffering by dynamically switching between different bitrates based on the available bandwidth.

The most common streaming protocols that support ABR are

Protocol	Description	Compatibility
HLS (HTTP Live Streaming)	Apple's proprietary protocol, widely used on iOS and MacOS	iOS, Safari, most browsers
DASH (Dynamic Adaptive Streaming over HTTP)	Open standard for ABR streaming	All modern browsers and platforms
RTMP (Real-Time Messaging Protocol)	Older protocol for live streaming	Flash-based players, some modern platforms

In an ABR setup, multiple versions of the video file are encoded at different bitrates. The video player monitors network conditions and device performance, switching between streams to provide the best possible viewing experience.

Building a Custom Video Player

The process of building a custom video player involves several technical steps

Loading the Media Source

The video player must load the media source from a local file, a CDN, or a streaming server. For web-based players, the <video> element in HTML5 is used to load and display video files.

Decoding and Rendering

Once the video file is loaded, the decoder processes the encoded video and audio streams. Hardware acceleration can be enabled to offload decoding to the GPU, improving performance and reducing CPU usage. The renderer then synchronizes the video frames and audio samples for smooth playback.

Buffering and Caching

A buffer is used to store video frames and audio samples before they are rendered. This prevents stuttering and interruptions due to network congestion.

User Interface and Controls

A custom UI provides playback controls, including play, pause, seek, volume adjustment, and fullscreen mode. Advanced features such as speed adjustment, picture-in-picture mode, and subtitle selection can also be integrated.

Performance Optimization

Performance optimization includes reducing latency, improving load times, and minimizing memory usage. Techniques such as lazy loading, hardware acceleration, and adaptive buffering improve overall performance.

Cross-Device and Platform Compatibility

Ensuring compatibility across different devices and platforms requires testing the video player on multiple browsers, operating systems, and screen resolutions. Responsive design techniques ensure that the video player adapts to different screen sizes and orientations.

Platform	Recommended Framework	Supported Codecs
Web	HTML5, JavaScript	H.264, VP9, AV1
Android	ExoPlayer	H.264, H.265, VP9
iOS	AVPlayer	H.264, H.265
Windows	DirectShow, Media Foundation	H.264, VP9, AV1
Linux	GStreamer	H.264, VP9, AV1

Building a custom video player requires careful consideration of supported codecs, streaming protocols, and platform compatibility. Adaptive bitrate streaming improves playback quality under varying network conditions, while performance optimizations ensure smooth playback and fast loading times. A responsive user interface enhances the viewing experience, while hardware acceleration and efficient buffering reduce resource consumption. The combination of an efficient architecture, broad codec support, and adaptive streaming ensures a high-quality video playback experience across all devices and platforms.

Chapter 8

Security and Privacy in Video Platforms

The growing popularity of video streaming platforms has made them a prime target for cyberattacks, piracy, and unauthorized access. As the volume of video content increases and the demand for high-quality, on-demand streaming rises, the need for robust security and privacy measures becomes more critical. Protecting video content from unauthorized access, safeguarding user data, and ensuring a secure streaming experience are fundamental to building trust with users and maintaining the integrity of the platform.

Security and privacy issues in video platforms are multifaceted. They involve protecting the video content itself, securing the transmission of video streams over the internet, controlling user access, and safeguarding the personal information of users. Without adequate security measures, video content is vulnerable to unauthorized downloads, screen recording, and redistribution, which can result in revenue loss and damage to the content creator's intellectual property. In addition, weak privacy controls can lead to data breaches, exposing sensitive user information such as login credentials, payment details, and viewing habits.

This chapter explores the key security and privacy challenges faced by video platforms, including piracy, unauthorized access, and data breaches. It examines the technical mechanisms available to protect video content, including encryption, digital rights management (DRM), and secure transmission protocols. It also addresses the importance of privacy policies, user consent, and data protection regulations to ensure compliance with legal standards and maintain user trust.

Threats and Challenges in Video Platform Security

Security threats to video platforms arise from both internal and external sources. External threats include hacking attempts, phishing attacks, denial-of-service (DoS) attacks, and piracy. Internal threats can result from misconfigured access controls, unintentional data leaks, and insider attacks.

One of the most common challenges is content piracy, where unauthorized parties capture, copy, and redistribute video content without permission. Piracy not only results in direct revenue loss but also undermines the content creator's intellectual property rights. Unauthorized screen recording, torrent sharing, and password sharing are among the most frequent methods of content piracy.

Another critical challenge is unauthorized access to the platform, where attackers attempt to gain access to user accounts or admin controls through brute force attacks, credential stuffing, and social engineering. Weak password policies and lack of two-factor authentication (2FA) make platforms vulnerable to these types of attacks.

Data breaches present another significant threat to video platforms. If personal user data such as email addresses, passwords, and payment information are exposed, it can lead to identity theft and financial fraud. Regulatory penalties and reputational damage often follow data breaches, making user data protection a top priority.

Encryption for Secure Content Transmission

Encryption is one of the most effective methods for securing video content during transmission and storage. Encryption converts video data into a scrambled format that can only be decrypted by authorized clients with the correct decryption key.

Types of Encryption for Video Platforms

Encryption can be applied at different levels, depending on the type of content and the streaming architecture. The most common encryption methods include

Encryption Type	Description	Use Case	Strength

Encryption Type	Description	Use Case	Strength
AES-128 (Advanced Encryption Standard)	Symmetric encryption standard with a 128-bit key	HLS and DASH streaming	High
AES-256	Stronger version of AES encryption with a 256-bit key	High-security content and DRM systems	Very High
TLS (Transport Layer Security)	Secures the transmission of video streams over HTTP	Live and on-demand streaming	Moderate
RSA (Rivest-Shamir-Adleman)	Asymmetric encryption for secure key exchange	DRM and secure login systems	High

AES-128 and AES-256 encryption are widely used in streaming protocols such as HLS (HTTP Live Streaming) and DASH (Dynamic Adaptive Streaming over HTTP). The encryption process involves generating a key that is securely distributed to the client. The video stream is encoded in small chunks, each protected with the encryption key.

TLS encryption is used to secure the connection between the client and the server, ensuring that video content and metadata are not intercepted or modified during transmission. RSA encryption is often used for key exchange in DRM systems, ensuring that only authenticated users can decrypt the video content.

Digital Rights Management (DRM)

Digital Rights Management (DRM) is a technology used to control access to digital content and prevent unauthorized copying and redistribution. DRM protects intellectual property by embedding encryption and access controls directly into the video file, making it difficult for unauthorized users to extract or modify the content.

How DRM Works

The DRM process involves three key components

Encryption – The video file is encrypted using AES or similar encryption standards.

License Server – A DRM license server issues decryption keys to authorized clients.

Player Integration – The video player integrates with the DRM system, validating the user's license before decoding the video stream.

The diagram below illustrates the DRM process

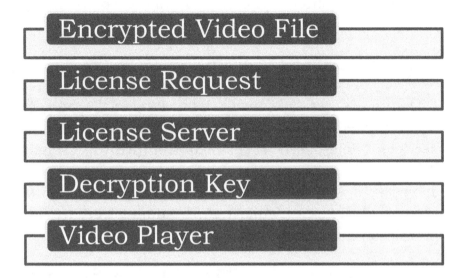

Common DRM Solutions

Several DRM solutions are widely used in the video streaming industry

DRM System	Developer	Supported Platforms
Widevine	Google	Chrome, Android, Smart TVs
PlayReady	Microsoft	Windows, Edge, Xbox
FairPlay	Apple	Safari, iOS, Apple TV

Widevine, PlayReady, and FairPlay provide end-to-end content protection by integrating encryption, key

83

management, and playback restrictions. Multi-DRM strategies are often employed to ensure compatibility across different platforms and devices.

Access Control and User Authentication

Effective access control mechanisms prevent unauthorized access to video content and platform services. Role-based access control (RBAC) assigns different levels of access to different user groups. For example, a standard user may have access only to video playback, while an administrator has permissions to upload and modify content.

Two-factor authentication (2FA) adds an extra layer of security by requiring a second form of verification, such as a one-time password (OTP) sent via email or SMS. OAuth and OpenID Connect (OIDC) protocols enable secure user authentication through third-party services such as Google, Facebook, and Apple.

Secure Session Management

Session management ensures that user sessions remain secure even when the user is logged in for an extended period. Secure cookies, token-based authentication, and automatic session expiration reduce the risk of session hijacking.

Prevention of Credential Stuffing

To prevent credential stuffing and brute force attacks, platforms should implement rate limiting, IP blocking, and CAPTCHA challenges for repeated login attempts. Password strength requirements and secure storage (e.g., hashing and salting) further enhance protection.

Privacy Policies and User Data Protection

Data privacy is essential for maintaining user trust and ensuring compliance with data protection regulations such as the General Data Protection Regulation (GDPR) and the California Consumer Privacy Act (CCPA). A clear and transparent privacy policy should outline how user data is collected, stored, and used.

User data protection measures include

Minimization of Data Collection – Collect only the data necessary for platform operation.

Encryption of User Data – Store user data using strong encryption standards.

Anonymization and Masking – Remove identifying information from user data to protect privacy.

User Consent and Opt-Out – Provide users with the ability to consent to data collection and opt out of targeted advertising.

A sample privacy policy structure is shown below

Section	Description
Data Collection	Types of data collected (e.g., email, payment details)
Data Usage	How data is used (e.g., recommendations, account management)
Third-Party Sharing	Disclosure of data to partners and advertisers
User Rights	Access, deletion, and correction of data

Securing a video platform requires a combination of encryption, DRM, access control, and user authentication. Encryption protects video streams from interception and tampering, while DRM ensures that only authorized users can access content. Robust authentication mechanisms prevent unauthorized access, and secure session management reduces the risk of session hijacking. Privacy policies and data protection measures are essential for maintaining user trust and ensuring compliance with legal requirements. A secure video platform not only protects content and user data but also enhances the overall user experience by providing a safe and reliable streaming environment.

Chapter 9

Monetization Strategies for Video Platforms

The success of a video platform is not solely defined by the quality of content or user engagement but also by its ability to generate consistent revenue. Monetization is at the core of any sustainable video platform, as it ensures that the platform remains operational, competitive, and capable of supporting content creators and platform maintenance costs. Monetization strategies for video platforms have evolved significantly with the rise of on-demand streaming, live broadcasts, and user-generated content. The ability to implement a successful monetization strategy requires a deep understanding of user behavior, market trends, and technical integration with payment systems and ad-server technologies.

Monetization models for video platforms can be broadly classified into three major categories advertising-based models, subscription-based models, and pay-per-view models. Each model comes with its own set of challenges and advantages, and successful video platforms often combine multiple strategies to maximize revenue. Advertising-based models rely on third-party advertisers who pay for ad placements within the platform's content. Subscription-based models provide a steady stream of revenue by charging users a recurring fee for access to premium content. Pay-per-view models allow users to purchase or rent specific pieces of content, providing flexibility in consumption patterns.

This chapter provides an in-depth examination of each monetization model, detailing the technical implementation, advantages, and potential challenges. It also explores the role of payment gateways, subscription management systems, and ad-serving platforms in enabling seamless monetization. By understanding these models and the technical requirements behind them, video platform owners can build scalable and profitable platforms.

Advertising-Based Monetization

Advertising-based monetization is one of the most widely used revenue models for video platforms. It involves displaying advertisements within the video player or around the platform interface and earning revenue from advertisers based on user engagement, impressions, or clicks. This model is particularly effective for platforms with large user bases and high viewing times.

Types of Advertising Models

Advertising-based monetization can take various forms depending on the format, placement, and interaction with the content. The most common advertising models include

Advertising Model	Description	Payment Structure	Example
Pre-roll Ads	Short ads displayed before the video starts	CPM (Cost per Mille), CPC (Cost per Click)	YouTube Pre-roll Ads
Mid-roll Ads	Ads inserted at intervals during video playback	CPM, CPC	Twitch Mid-stream Ads
Post-roll Ads	Ads displayed after the video ends	CPM, CPC	Hulu Post-roll Ads
Overlay Ads	Semi-transparent ads overlaid on the video screen	CPM, CPC	YouTube Overlay Ads
Sponsored Content	Advertiser-funded content integrated into the platform	Fixed fee or revenue share	Influencer Videos
Native Ads	Ads blended into the platform interface (e.g., recommended videos)	CPM, CPC	Facebook Video Feed Ads

Pre-roll, mid-roll, and post-roll ads are the most common ad placements used in video platforms. Pre-roll ads typically have higher completion rates because they are shown before the user starts watching the content. Mid-roll ads are effective for longer videos, but they can disrupt the viewing experience if not timed properly. Post-roll ads have lower engagement rates but can be effective when combined with calls to action (e.g., "Watch Next" or "Subscribe").

Ad-Server Integration

To implement an advertising-based model, video platforms need to integrate with an ad-serving platform such as Google AdSense, DoubleClick, or third-party programmatic ad networks. The ad server delivers ads based on user demographics, geographic location, browsing history, and device type.

The following diagram illustrates how ad-serving integration works

Ad-serving platforms use real-time bidding (RTB) to auction ad slots to advertisers. When a user requests to watch a video, the platform sends a request to the ad server. The ad server holds a real-time auction where advertisers bid for the ad slot. The highest bidder's ad is then displayed to the user.

Ad targeting strategies enhance revenue generation by increasing the relevance of ads to users. Behavioral targeting (based on browsing history), contextual targeting (based on video content), and geographic targeting (based on location) increase engagement rates and maximize CPM and CPC earnings.

Subscription-Based Monetization

Subscription-based monetization is a direct-to-consumer model where users pay a recurring fee (monthly, quarterly, or annually) for access to premium content. This model generates predictable revenue streams and fosters user loyalty by offering exclusive content and an ad-free experience.

Types of Subscription Models

Subscription models vary based on the type of content offered and the level of access granted to users.

Subscription Model	Description	Example
SVOD (Subscription Video on Demand)	Unlimited access to a library of content for a fixed monthly fee	Netflix, Disney+
TVOD (Transactional Video on Demand)	Pay-per-title rental or purchase with a subscription option for bundled content	Amazon Prime Video
Hybrid Subscription	Combination of SVOD and TVOD models, where users can access basic content for free and pay for premium content	Hulu, YouTube Premium
Tiered Subscription	Different subscription levels offering varying degrees of access and benefits	Spotify Premium, Netflix (Basic, Standard, Premium)

SVOD platforms like Netflix and Disney+ rely on high-quality content libraries and original programming to attract and retain subscribers. TVOD platforms such as Amazon Prime Video offer flexibility by allowing users to rent or purchase individual titles without a subscription. Hybrid models like Hulu offer ad-supported basic plans with an option to upgrade to an ad-free experience.

Subscription Management Systems

Implementing a subscription model requires a robust subscription management system capable of handling user registration, billing, renewal, and cancellations.

Subscription platforms integrate with payment gateways like Stripe, PayPal, and Apple Pay to process recurring payments securely. The subscription management system assigns user permissions based on the subscription tier and manages renewals and cancellations automatically.

Auto-renewals improve user retention rates, while offering incentives like free trials and discounted rates can increase subscriber acquisition.

Pay-Per-View Monetization

Pay-per-view (PPV) monetization allows users to purchase or rent individual pieces of content without committing to a subscription. This model is effective for live events, sports broadcasts, and newly released movies.

How Pay-Per-View Works

In a pay-per-view model, users pay for temporary or permanent access to a specific piece of content. Temporary access usually allows the user to stream the content for a limited period (e.g., 24–48 hours). Permanent access allows the user to download or stream the content indefinitely.

Pay-Per-View Type	Description	Example
Single Rental	One-time payment for temporary access	UFC Fight Pass
Permanent Purchase	One-time payment for lifetime access	iTunes Movie Purchase
Event Ticketing	Pay-per-event access for live streaming	WWE Network

Pay-per-view models require integration with a secure payment gateway and content delivery network (CDN) to manage high traffic volumes during live events. Secure token-based access prevents unauthorized sharing of PPV content.

Payment Gateway Integration

Payment gateway integration is essential for processing subscription fees, pay-per-view purchases, and ad revenue payouts. Payment gateways such as Stripe, PayPal, and Braintree handle payment processing, currency conversion, and fraud detection.

Payment Processing Workflow

The payment processing workflow involves

Payment gateways support multiple currencies, tax calculations, and refunds, providing a seamless user experience. Secure Socket Layer (SSL) encryption ensures that payment details are protected during transmission.

A successful monetization strategy for video platforms involves a balanced combination of advertising, subscriptions, and pay-per-view models. Advertising-based models leverage targeted ads to generate revenue from high user traffic. Subscription-based models provide predictable revenue streams and foster user loyalty. Pay-per-view models offer flexibility for premium and event-based content. Secure payment gateway integration and subscription management systems are essential for processing transactions and managing user access. A well-executed monetization strategy ensures sustainable growth, profitability, and long-term user satisfaction.

Chapter 10

AI and Machine Learning in Video Platforms

Artificial Intelligence (AI) and Machine Learning (ML) are revolutionizing the way video platforms function, enhancing user experiences, improving content management, and driving platform efficiency. From personalized video recommendations to automated content moderation and intelligent video analysis, the integration of AI and machine learning in video platforms is transforming every aspect of video consumption. By leveraging these technologies, platforms can streamline workflows, increase user engagement, reduce operational costs, and create more personalized and secure environments for users.

In this chapter, we will delve into the critical roles AI and machine learning play in video platforms, exploring their application in areas such as content recommendation systems, automatic content moderation, and video analysis. Additionally, we will discuss how to integrate machine learning models into video processing workflows to enable automation, improve decision-making, and optimize the overall user experience.

Video Recommendation Systems

One of the most prominent applications of AI and machine learning in video platforms is the development of video recommendation systems. These systems are designed to analyze user behavior, preferences, and interactions with content to suggest videos that are most likely to engage the user. The goal is to create a personalized experience that keeps users engaged and increases time spent on the platform.

How Video Recommendation Systems Work

Recommendation systems generally rely on algorithms that analyze historical user data, including watch history, likes, shares, and searches, to predict the content that a user will be most interested in. Machine learning models can process this data in real-time to provide highly relevant video suggestions. Some common recommendation system techniques include

Collaborative Filtering

Collaborative filtering is based on the idea that users who have liked similar videos in the past are likely to enjoy similar content in the future. There are two types of collaborative filtering techniques user-based and item-based. User-based filtering identifies users with similar interests and recommends content based on what other similar users have watched. Item-based filtering looks at videos that are similar to those a user has previously watched, recommending videos based on similarities in content.

Content-Based Filtering

Content-based filtering focuses on the features of the videos themselves. This method analyzes the metadata of videos—such as titles, descriptions, tags, and even visual and audio features—and matches them with user preferences. For example, if a user regularly watches action-packed thrillers, the system will recommend videos with similar themes, genres, or keywords.

Hybrid Approaches

Hybrid recommendation systems combine collaborative filtering and content-based filtering to leverage the strengths of both techniques. By integrating these approaches, hybrid models can provide more accurate and diverse recommendations, mitigating the limitations of each individual approach.

Machine Learning Models

Machine learning algorithms, such as decision trees, k-nearest neighbors (k-NN), and matrix factorization, can be used to build recommendation systems. Deep learning models, particularly neural networks, have become increasingly popular for building more sophisticated recommendation engines. For example, recurrent neural networks (RNNs) and convolutional neural networks (CNNs) can analyze sequential patterns in user behavior and video content to generate more personalized and accurate recommendations.

The process of integrating these models into a video platform often involves gathering vast amounts of user interaction data, training models on this data, and then deploying the trained models into the platform's backend to deliver real-time video recommendations. As user behavior evolves, continuous training of these models is necessary to adapt to new trends and content preferences.

Automatic Content Moderation

With the exponential growth of user-generated content on video platforms, maintaining a safe and respectful environment has become more challenging. Manual content moderation is time-consuming and often inadequate, especially for platforms with millions of videos uploaded daily. AI and machine learning offer scalable solutions to automatically identify and remove harmful or inappropriate content, ensuring that platforms adhere to community guidelines and legal standards.

How Automatic Content Moderation Works

AI-based content moderation leverages machine learning models trained to detect inappropriate content such as nudity, violence, hate speech, and other forms of harmful behavior. These models are typically trained on large datasets of labeled content to learn the characteristics of unwanted videos.

Image and Video Recognition

Computer vision algorithms are used to analyze the visual content of videos, detecting explicit or violent imagery. Convolutional neural networks (CNNs) are commonly used in this process, as they are capable of recognizing objects, scenes, and faces in images. For example, CNNs can detect inappropriate symbols, gestures, or explicit material in videos.

Natural Language Processing (NLP) for Speech

Natural Language Processing (NLP) is used to analyze the audio and text content in videos, including subtitles, descriptions, and comments. NLP models are trained to identify hate speech, offensive language, or other harmful text in spoken or written form. These models can detect harmful keywords or phrases and flag them for moderation.

Sentiment Analysis

Sentiment analysis can be used to assess the emotional tone of content. AI models trained to perform sentiment analysis can identify content that might be aggressive or inflammatory based on the language used. This is particularly useful for moderating user comments and ensuring that interactions within the platform remain respectful.

Challenges in Content Moderation

Despite its effectiveness, automatic content moderation comes with its own challenges. AI models can sometimes make mistakes, flagging non-offensive content or missing harmful content. False positives (inaccurately identifying harmful content) and false negatives (failing to identify harmful content) are common issues. To mitigate these challenges, AI-driven content moderation is often combined with human oversight. This hybrid approach ensures that AI systems can quickly filter out obvious violations, while human moderators step in to handle more complex cases.

Video Analysis and Metadata Extraction

AI and machine learning can also be used to extract meaningful metadata from video content, enabling better content management, searchability, and indexing. Video platforms rely on AI-driven video analysis to tag, categorize, and analyze content in ways that were previously impossible with manual methods.

Key Areas of Video Analysis

Video analysis refers to the extraction of information from video content, such as detecting objects, scenes, actions, and even emotions. Some common video analysis techniques include

Object Detection

AI-powered object detection algorithms identify and classify objects within video frames. This can be applied to various scenarios, such as identifying products in an e-commerce video, detecting vehicles in a surveillance feed, or recognizing faces in a social media video.

Scene Recognition

AI models trained to recognize specific scenes within a video (e.g., indoors, outdoors, cityscape) can automatically categorize content. This is useful for creating content libraries, tagging videos by location or theme, and improving searchability.

Action Recognition

In action recognition, machine learning models are used to analyze movements or behaviors within videos. This is particularly useful for sports video analysis, where specific actions, such as a goal being scored or a player performing a skill, can be tagged and categorized for easy access.

Speech-to-Text and Captioning

Speech recognition and transcription services powered by machine learning can generate captions or subtitles for videos in real-time, improving accessibility and enabling better content searchability.

Benefits of Video Analysis

The integration of video analysis into a video platform allows for more accurate content indexing, better search results, and automated content categorization. Additionally, it enables personalized recommendations by analyzing the specific characteristics of the video content that users interact with.

Machine Learning into Video Processing

To fully leverage AI and machine learning capabilities, video platforms must integrate these technologies into their video processing workflows. Machine learning models can be applied at various stages of video processing, including encoding, storage, and playback.

In the workflow, machine learning models can be used during the pre-processing stage to automatically categorize and tag videos based on their content. Once videos are indexed and categorized, the recommendation system can use machine learning to predict which videos are most likely to engage the user. Additionally, content moderation models can be applied before the video is made public, ensuring that harmful content is filtered out in real-time.

AI and machine learning have the potential to completely transform the way video platforms operate. By integrating intelligent recommendation systems, automatic content moderation, and video analysis, video platforms can offer more personalized, secure, and engaging user experiences. Furthermore, the ability to incorporate machine learning models into video processing workflows not only enhances efficiency but also opens up new possibilities for content discovery, categorization, and user interaction. With the right implementation, AI can play a central role in driving growth, improving user retention, and creating more effective content strategies for video platforms.

Chapter 11

Virtual Reality (VR) and Augmented Reality (AR) Integration

The integration of Virtual Reality (VR) and Augmented Reality (AR) technologies into video platforms represents the next frontier in creating immersive and interactive video experiences. As these technologies continue to evolve, they offer unprecedented opportunities to transform the way users engage with video content, providing new ways to experience entertainment, education, training, and more. In this chapter, we will explore the future of immersive video experiences through VR and AR, discuss how to develop platforms that support 360-degree videos, interactive VR content, and augmented reality layers, and understand the technical aspects of integrating these immersive experiences into video platforms.

Virtual Reality (VR) and Its Role in Video Platforms

Virtual Reality refers to a fully immersive, computer-generated environment that can simulate the real world or create entirely fantastical worlds. Unlike traditional video experiences, where users passively watch content on a screen, VR enables users to interact with and explore a fully immersive 3D space. This shift from passive viewing to active participation is one of the key features that make VR such a powerful tool for video platforms.

Key Components of VR Content

Creating compelling VR experiences requires careful consideration of several technical components

360-Degree Video

A core component of VR content is 360-degree video. These videos capture the entire environment in every direction, allowing users to look around and explore the scene. This type of video is typically shot with a specialized camera that records in all directions simultaneously, or with multiple cameras stitched together to create a spherical image. When viewed in VR headsets, the video becomes a fully immersive experience, with users able to look in any direction as if they were physically present in the scene.

360-degree video can be used for a wide range of applications, from virtual tourism and live event broadcasting to training simulations and entertainment. The integration of 360-degree video in a VR platform involves stitching video footage into a single spherical image, rendering the content in real time, and ensuring that it responds to the user's head movements within the VR environment.

Interactive VR Content

One of the key differentiators of VR content from traditional video is interactivity. VR allows users to not just observe the content but actively engage with it. This interactivity can come in many forms, such as allowing users to navigate through a virtual world, interact with objects within the environment, or make decisions that affect the outcome of the experience.

Developing interactive VR content requires the integration of game engines like Unity or Unreal Engine, which support the creation of 3D environments and interactive elements. These engines also allow for the incorporation of features like physics simulations, realistic lighting, and collision detection, enhancing the sense of presence and realism in the VR experience.

Immersion and Presence

The feeling of presence, or being physically "inside" the virtual environment, is critical to a successful VR experience. To achieve this, VR platforms rely on several technologies, including stereoscopic 3D rendering (creating the illusion of depth), spatial audio (providing directionality to sounds within the environment), and head tracking (allowing the system to update the view based on the user's head movements).

Developing VR Platforms for Video

Creating a VR platform that supports immersive content involves several considerations beyond just the creation of 360-degree videos and interactive elements. The platform needs to provide seamless playback, high-quality rendering, low latency, and compatibility with various VR headsets.

Content Delivery and Streaming

Streaming VR content requires high-bandwidth connections, especially when delivering 360-degree video at high resolutions such as 4K or 8K. The content needs to be delivered with low latency to avoid motion sickness, a common issue in VR experiences. Adaptive bitrate streaming, where the video quality dynamically adjusts based on the user's internet connection, is often used to ensure smooth playback without interruptions.

VR Hardware Integration

The VR platform must also integrate with various hardware devices, including headsets (such as Oculus Rift, HTC Vive, or PlayStation VR), controllers, and motion tracking devices. The platform should support different interaction models, including hand tracking, voice commands, and physical controllers, to provide a fully immersive experience.

Augmented Reality (AR) and Its Role

While VR immerses users in entirely digital environments, Augmented Reality blends the virtual world with the real world. AR enhances the user's perception of their surroundings by overlaying digital content (such as images, sounds, or videos) onto real-world environments in real-time. The key advantage of AR is that it allows users to interact with both virtual and real-world elements simultaneously, creating interactive and dynamic video experiences.

Key Components of AR Content

AR Layers and Visual Overlays

In AR, digital elements (e.g., 3D models, animations, text, or video content) are overlaid onto the real-world view through a camera or a display. This is often done in real-time using the device's camera to capture the environment and computer vision algorithms to detect surfaces and objects in the scene. AR layers can enhance video content by adding contextual information, interactivity, or even gamified elements. For example, during a live sports broadcast, an AR layer could display player statistics or a live score overlay.

Interactive AR Experiences

One of the most engaging features of AR is its ability to enable interaction between the user and the digital elements. For example, users might be able to point their phone at a physical object to reveal additional content, such as videos, animations, or detailed information about that object. Interactive AR content is commonly used in mobile applications, but with the advent of AR glasses (such as Microsoft HoloLens or Magic Leap), AR is poised to move beyond mobile devices and become more integrated into everyday experiences.

Tracking and Mapping

For AR content to be accurately placed in the real world, the platform needs to track the user's environment and the user's position within that environment. This involves advanced computer vision techniques that can detect and map physical spaces, such as detecting walls, floors, and objects, to ensure that AR content is placed realistically within the environment. This can be done through techniques such as simultaneous localization and mapping (SLAM), which allows the AR system to track the movement of both the user and the environment.

Developing AR Platforms for Video

The integration of AR into video platforms involves multiple stages, from content creation to rendering and interaction. To develop a platform that supports AR video content, the following components are necessary

AR Content Creation

Creating AR content requires specialized tools and software, such as ARKit (for iOS) or ARCore (for Android), which provide the necessary frameworks for developing AR experiences. Additionally, 3D modeling software (such as Blender or Autodesk Maya) is used to create the virtual objects that will be overlaid onto the real world. These models are then integrated into the AR experience, with their behavior and interactions defined using game engines or AR development platforms.

Real-Time Rendering

Like VR, AR video experiences need to be rendered in real-time to provide a seamless and immersive experience. This requires high-performance graphics rendering, with the AR system dynamically updating the video content to respond to changes in the user's environment. Low latency is also essential to ensure that the AR elements stay synchronized with the real-world view, especially when the user is moving around.

Hardware and Device Integration

AR platforms need to integrate with devices that support AR functionality, such as smartphones, tablets, or AR glasses. These devices must have the necessary hardware to support the AR experience, including cameras, depth sensors, and accelerometers. Furthermore, the platform needs to optimize for various screen sizes and device capabilities to ensure a consistent experience across devices.

Future of VR and AR in Video Platforms

The future of VR and AR in video platforms is incredibly promising, with several emerging trends likely to shape their evolution

Improved Hardware

As VR and AR hardware continues to improve, we can expect more powerful and lightweight headsets, along with more advanced AR glasses that offer greater immersion and comfort. These advancements will make it easier for consumers to engage with immersive content for longer periods without experiencing discomfort.

Enhanced Content Creation Tools

The development of more intuitive and accessible content creation tools will lower the barrier to entry for developers and content creators, making it easier to produce high-quality VR and AR content. These tools will enable more diverse and innovative experiences, from interactive 360-degree videos to complex AR video games and simulations.

Integration with 5G Networks

The rollout of 5G networks will significantly improve the delivery of high-quality VR and AR content by reducing latency and increasing bandwidth. This will enable smoother streaming of 360-degree video and interactive AR experiences, allowing for real-time engagement without the limitations of current network speeds.

Social VR and AR

As VR and AR technologies evolve, we may see the rise of social platforms that allow users to interact with each other in virtual and augmented environments. These platforms could combine video streaming, gaming, and social networking, enabling users to share experiences in new and interactive ways.

The integration of Virtual Reality and Augmented Reality into video platforms is paving the way for the future of immersive video experiences. As VR allows users to explore 360-degree environments and interact with content in real-time, and AR enhances real-world environments with digital overlays, these technologies are revolutionizing the way we experience video. With advancements in hardware, content creation tools, and network capabilities, VR and AR are set to redefine entertainment, education, and communication. Video platforms that successfully integrate these immersive technologies will be at the forefront of this exciting new era of interactive content.

Chapter 12

Edge Computing for Video Delivery

The increasing demand for high-quality video content, particularly through streaming platforms, has necessitated advancements in technology to ensure seamless delivery. One of the key innovations in video delivery systems is **edge computing**. This technology has revolutionized the way video content is distributed across networks, offering substantial improvements in performance, reduced latency, and more efficient use of resources. As viewers expect uninterrupted, high-quality streaming experiences, especially in real-time applications like live broadcasting, gaming, and interactive video platforms, traditional content delivery systems, based on central servers, often fall short in meeting these needs. Edge computing solves these challenges by bringing computation closer to the user.

In this chapter, we will explore how edge computing can optimize video delivery, reduce latency, and improve performance. We will also dive into the specific methods of **video caching at the edge** and how this technology enables localized content delivery. Through this, we aim to provide a comprehensive understanding of edge computing's role in transforming the video streaming ecosystem and its implementation.

Introduction to Edge Computing in Video Delivery

Edge computing refers to the practice of processing data closer to the location where it is being generated rather than relying solely on centralized data centers. This decentralization of computation helps in reducing the distance that data needs to travel, which leads to faster processing times, lower latency, and a more responsive user experience. In the context of video delivery, edge computing improves the overall streaming performance by reducing the time it takes to request and retrieve video data, especially for content-heavy applications like video-on-demand (VOD) services or live video streaming.

The Role of Edge Computing

In traditional content delivery networks (CDNs), video content is delivered from centralized servers that are typically located in a few data centers spread across regions. While this works well for general purposes, as demand for high-definition and 4K video content grows, along with real-time interactive experiences such as virtual reality (VR) and augmented reality (AR), these systems face several limitations. The primary issues include high latency, network congestion, and the inability to efficiently handle sudden spikes in demand.

Edge computing addresses these issues by moving computational resources, such as video processing and caching, closer to the **edge** of the network, where users are located. This allows video content to be cached locally, significantly reducing the time it takes to deliver the video to the user. By reducing the number of hops data must make over the internet, edge computing minimizes the distance between the user and the server, thus reducing **latency** and improving the overall quality of experience.

Key Benefits of Edge Computing

Edge computing offers several advantages for video delivery

Reduced Latency

By storing video data closer to the user, edge computing drastically reduces latency. This is particularly crucial for applications like live video streaming, online gaming, and video conferencing, where delays in transmission can lead to poor user experiences, stuttering video, or even disconnections.

Improved Performance and Quality

Edge computing ensures that video streams are delivered without buffering and with minimal interruptions. By leveraging local caching, video streams can be delivered with high quality, even during periods of high demand. Moreover, edge computing systems can provide a smoother experience for users by adapting the quality of the video based on their connection speeds, further reducing buffering times.

Scalability and Load Distribution

Edge computing helps distribute traffic more effectively by balancing the load across multiple edge nodes. This enhances the scalability of the video delivery system and allows it to handle a larger number of users, especially during peak traffic periods, without significant performance degradation.

Optimized Network Utilization

Since video data is cached at the edge, fewer requests need to travel all the way back to the central server. This reduces the amount of traffic over long-distance routes, optimizing the use of network bandwidth. In turn, this reduces the potential for network congestion, ensuring that video content is delivered more efficiently.

Implementing Video Caching at the Edge

One of the most significant applications of edge computing in video delivery is **video caching at the edge**. Caching video content at the edge of the network allows video streaming platforms to store frequently accessed content closer to the user, thus improving access times and reducing the load on centralized servers.

Video Caching Techniques

Video caching can be broken down into different techniques, which depend on the type of content and how frequently it is accessed. Caching mechanisms involve storing content temporarily in local storage at edge servers, which is then retrieved when requested by a user. The primary strategies for video caching include

Content-based Caching

This technique involves caching popular video content based on demand. When a large number of users request the same video, it is cached at the edge node closest to those users. Content-based caching ensures that high-demand videos are readily available for fast delivery. For example, a live sports broadcast or viral video would be cached at local edge nodes to reduce the time it takes to deliver the content to users in a particular geographical area.

Time-based Caching

Time-based caching is useful for live events or video streams that are only relevant for a specific time frame. Content is cached at the edge for a limited period, such as the duration of a sports event, concert, or conference. Once the event is over, the content is removed from the cache to free up storage space for new content.

Pre-fetching and Predictive Caching

Pre-fetching involves predicting what content will be requested next based on user behavior, viewing history, or seasonal trends. By anticipating demand, the system pre-caches content before it is actually requested, ensuring that the content is available at the edge when users need it. For instance, if a new episode of a popular series is about to be released, the system can pre-fetch that episode and store it at the edge to avoid buffering during peak viewership.

Adaptive Caching

Adaptive caching involves dynamically adjusting the caching strategy based on real-time data. For example, if a particular video is gaining unexpected popularity, the system might prioritize caching it at edge servers closer to regions with higher demand. Adaptive caching helps optimize resource allocation, ensuring that popular videos are always available, while less-demanded videos are removed from caches to make room for more relevant content.

Localized Content Delivery

One of the most significant advantages of edge computing in video delivery is **localized content delivery**. Edge computing enables the delivery of video content from servers that are geographically closer to the end user, rather than relying on distant data centers. This reduces network congestion and ensures faster delivery times.

Localized content delivery also allows video platforms to provide region-specific content or even tailor video streams based on localized preferences and requirements. For example, a user in Japan might be served localized video content with Japanese subtitles, while a user in the United States receives content with English subtitles.

Edge computing also facilitates the **dynamic allocation of resources** based on local traffic patterns. If an edge node experiences high demand from users in a specific region, additional resources can be provisioned dynamically to handle the load.

This ensures that content is delivered efficiently, even during peak usage periods.

Handling Latency and Redundancy

Although edge computing offers significant performance benefits, there are also challenges in maintaining consistent performance across a distributed network. Managing latency and redundancy are crucial factors to consider when implementing video delivery systems that leverage edge computing.

Minimizing Latency

Latency is one of the most critical factors in video delivery. The primary challenge in minimizing latency is ensuring that the video content is delivered in real-time or with minimal delay. Edge computing reduces latency by storing video content closer to the user, but maintaining low latency requires careful management of data routes and cache expiration policies. Optimizing video content delivery networks and reducing the number of hops in the network can further minimize latency.

Redundancy for Reliability

Redundancy is another key consideration in edge video delivery. Ensuring that content is available at all times, even if one edge server goes offline, requires deploying multiple edge servers and employing failover mechanisms. Redundancy is achieved by distributing video content across several edge nodes, with each node capable of taking over delivery in case another node fails.

To ensure reliable delivery, video platforms may implement **multi-CDN strategies**, where multiple CDNs (Content Delivery Networks) collaborate to handle video traffic, providing redundancy and optimizing content delivery.

Future of Edge Computing in Video Delivery

Edge computing is poised to play an increasingly important role in the future of video streaming, as the demand for high-quality content continues to grow. The continuous advancements in edge technologies, coupled with the proliferation of **5G networks**, will further enhance the ability to deliver video content with ultra-low latency and high performance. As video streaming platforms evolve, they will rely more heavily on edge computing to deliver personalized, localized, and real-time content, creating more immersive experiences for users.

In conclusion, edge computing is a transformative technology that has the potential to significantly enhance video delivery systems by reducing latency, improving performance, and enabling efficient, localized content delivery. By leveraging video caching at the edge and optimizing the use of network resources, edge computing helps deliver high-quality video content with reduced buffering and faster load times. As this technology continues to evolve, edge computing will become an essential tool for video platforms, ensuring that they can meet the growing demands of users for high-definition, real-time, and interactive video experiences.

Chapter 13

The Future of Video Platforms Innovations and Trends

As the demand for video content continues to grow exponentially, the video streaming landscape is undergoing constant transformation. Over the past few decades, we have witnessed the shift from standard-definition content to high-definition (HD), 4K resolution, and now the early adoption of 8K technology. This technological evolution, coupled with innovations in artificial intelligence (AI), blockchain, and other cutting-edge technologies, is paving the way for the next generation of video platforms. These innovations have the potential to significantly impact the way content is created, distributed, and consumed. In this chapter, we will dive into some of the emerging trends and technologies that will shape the future of video platforms, including **8K video**, **AI-generated content**, **holographic video**, and **blockchain-based video distribution**. By exploring these technologies and their integration into video platforms, we can gain insight into how the video streaming experience will evolve over the coming years.

The Rise of 8K Video A New Era of Resolution

8K video, with a resolution of 7680 x 4320 pixels, represents the next frontier in video quality. While 4K and 1080p resolutions are still the standard for many video platforms, 8K video promises to bring an unprecedented level of detail and realism to the viewing experience. The increase in resolution is not merely about offering more pixels; it has profound implications for the way content is produced, delivered, and consumed.

The Impact of 8K on Content Creation

Content creators will need new tools and technologies to take full advantage of 8K resolution. Cameras capable of capturing 8K footage are already available, and production studios are beginning to adopt these technologies to create ultra-high-definition content. However, 8K video requires significantly more storage, processing power, and bandwidth than 4K or 1080p content. To address these challenges, video platforms will need to invest in more efficient encoding and compression algorithms to ensure that 8K content can be delivered seamlessly to users.

Challenges in 8K Video Delivery

Streaming 8K video will demand massive amounts of bandwidth, which could prove challenging for current internet infrastructures. With most consumers relying on broadband connections with speeds far lower than what is required for 8K streaming, widespread adoption will be gradual. To mitigate this, video platforms may need to leverage technologies like **adaptive bitrate streaming** and **edge computing** to optimize the delivery of 8K content, ensuring that users with slower internet connections can still enjoy high-quality video at a lower resolution without buffering.

Additionally, **5G networks** are expected to play a crucial role in the delivery of 8K video, providing the necessary bandwidth and low latency for real-time streaming of high-resolution content. As 5G infrastructure becomes more widespread, we can expect 8K video to become more mainstream, especially for live events, gaming, and immersive experiences like virtual reality (VR).

8K Video in Consumer Devices

The adoption of 8K video will also require advancements in consumer devices, such as televisions, smartphones, and VR headsets. Major television manufacturers are already rolling out 8K TVs, but the high cost and limited availability of 8K content have hindered mass adoption. However, as more content becomes available, and as the cost of 8K displays decreases, the demand for 8K-capable devices will likely grow.

AI-Generated Content Creation

Artificial intelligence (AI) is playing an increasingly significant role in content creation, and its potential to reshape the video industry is immense. AI-generated

135

content refers to video that is produced by algorithms, often with little or no human input. This can range from fully AI-generated films and television shows to smaller, more personalized pieces of content such as advertisements or social media videos.

AI for Video Editing and Production

AI can assist content creators by automating many of the tedious and time-consuming tasks associated with video editing. This includes tasks such as color grading, audio enhancement, and even scriptwriting. AI-driven tools like Adobe's Sensei and OpenAI's GPT series are already being used in video production to create and enhance content more efficiently. These tools can analyze raw footage and apply effects, transitions, and edits in a manner that mimics human creativity.

AI can also automate video editing processes like scene detection, object tracking, and facial recognition. This is particularly useful for large-scale video productions where time and resources are limited, allowing editors to focus more on creative decision-making.

Personalized AI-Generated Content

One of the most exciting applications of AI in video platforms is the creation of personalized video content. With AI, video platforms can analyze user data, such as viewing history, preferences, and demographic information, to generate videos tailored to individual users. For instance, an AI system might create personalized summaries of long-form videos or curate specific sections of content to highlight based on the user's interests. This could revolutionize the way users interact with video content, making the experience more engaging and relevant.

Deepfake Technology

While AI-generated content holds tremendous potential, it also raises important ethical concerns. **Deepfake technology**, which uses AI to create hyper-realistic, manipulated videos, has been a source of controversy, particularly in its use for creating fake news, disinformation, and harmful content. Video platforms will need to implement robust safeguards and AI-driven moderation systems to detect and prevent malicious uses of AI-generated content, ensuring that ethical standards are upheld.

Holographic Video

Holographic video technology offers the potential for a truly immersive video experience, allowing users to experience content in 3D and interact with it as though it were physically present. This technology has been popularized in science fiction, but recent advancements are making it increasingly feasible for real-world applications.

Holographic Video and Virtual Reality (VR)

Holographic video can be seen as the next step in the evolution of VR. While VR immerses users in a completely virtual environment, holographic video brings elements of reality into the digital realm, enabling lifelike, three-dimensional images that can be viewed from any angle. Unlike traditional 3D video, which requires special glasses, holographic video can be viewed with the naked eye, offering a more natural and immersive experience.

Applications in Entertainment

The potential applications for holographic video are vast. In the entertainment industry, it could be used for live performances, allowing audiences to experience concerts or theater performances from the comfort of their homes. It could also be utilized for virtual tourism, allowing users to experience destinations in 3D without leaving their homes.

In communications, holographic video could revolutionize video conferencing by providing a more lifelike and engaging experience. This would be especially beneficial for remote work, enabling more effective collaboration and communication in a 3D virtual space.

Challenges in Holographic Video Production

While holographic video holds great promise, there are significant challenges to overcome. First and foremost is the technology required to capture and display holographic images. Current displays capable of rendering 3D holograms are bulky and expensive, and creating high-quality holographic content requires specialized cameras and rendering software. Furthermore, the bandwidth required to stream holographic video is much higher than that of traditional video, which presents logistical challenges in terms of data transmission and storage.

Blockchain-Based Video Distribution

Blockchain technology, which is most commonly associated with cryptocurrencies, has potential far beyond digital currencies. One of the most exciting applications for blockchain is in video content distribution. Traditional video platforms rely on centralized servers and third-party services to host and distribute content. This creates challenges around content ownership, copyright infringement, and revenue distribution. Blockchain-based video distribution platforms aim to address these issues by creating decentralized, transparent systems that empower content creators and consumers alike.

Blockchain and Smart Contracts

Blockchain enables the use of **smart contracts**, which are self-executing contracts with the terms of the agreement directly written into code. In the context of video platforms, smart contracts can automate royalty payments, ensuring that creators are paid fairly for their work. By tracking every transaction and content consumption on the blockchain, these platforms offer a more transparent and equitable system for content monetization.

Decentralized Content Hosting

With blockchain, video content can be hosted across a decentralized network of nodes, rather than relying on a single centralized server. This reduces the risk of censorship, enhances privacy, and provides more control to the content creator. By removing intermediaries, blockchain also lowers distribution costs and opens the door to more direct creator-to-consumer interactions.

Challenges and Adoption

While blockchain has tremendous potential, it is still in the early stages of adoption for video platforms. The technology faces scalability challenges, and its integration into existing video streaming platforms would require significant changes to the underlying infrastructure. Additionally, the energy consumption associated with blockchain, particularly in proof-of-work systems, remains a concern. However, with advancements in blockchain scalability and energy efficiency, these issues may be mitigated in the future.

The Future of Video Platforms

As we look toward the future of video platforms, the landscape is set to be shaped by exciting innovations such as **8K video**, **AI-generated content**, **holographic video**, and **blockchain-based distribution**. These technologies promise to revolutionize the way content is created, consumed, and shared. However, as with any new technology, there are challenges to overcome, including infrastructure limitations, high costs, and ethical concerns. Nevertheless, the continued advancements in these areas are poised to unlock new possibilities for immersive, personalized, and decentralized video experiences that will transform the video streaming industry. By embracing these innovations, video platforms can stay ahead of the curve and offer users an unparalleled viewing experience.

Chapter 14

Practical Guide to Building a Video Platform

Creating a video platform from scratch is a comprehensive process that involves several critical components, including server setup, video encoding, building a video player, and implementing streaming services. This chapter provides a hands-on guide for those interested in creating their own video platform, focusing on essential aspects that will equip you with the skills and knowledge needed to develop and deploy a fully functional platform. Whether you're aiming to build a small, private platform for personal use or preparing for a more scalable, commercial video streaming service, this chapter will walk you through the process step by step.

Architecture of a Video Platform

Before diving into the practical steps, it's essential to understand the overall architecture of a video platform. At the core of any video platform lies a few fundamental building blocks

Frontend This is the user interface (UI) through which users interact with the platform. It consists of a web or mobile app, video player, user authentication system, and content management interface.

Backend This is the server-side infrastructure where all video content is stored, processed, and served to users. It includes media storage, video processing (encoding, transcoding), databases, and the streaming server.

Streaming Protocol This is the technology used to deliver video content to end-users efficiently. Common protocols include HTTP Live Streaming (HLS), Dynamic Adaptive Streaming over HTTP (DASH), and Real-Time Messaging Protocol (RTMP).

In this chapter, we'll break down each component, explain how to set it up, and walk you through the tools required to make it all work.

Setting Up the Servers and Hosting

The first step in building a video platform is setting up a reliable server infrastructure. Since video files are large, the platform needs to be scalable and capable of handling high traffic, especially if you're planning to deliver high-definition or 4K content. Let's go through the basics of setting up both the **backend server** and **media storage**.

Choosing the Right Hosting Solution

The hosting solution you choose will depend on the scale of your platform. For small-scale personal projects, a **cloud-based service** such as Amazon Web Services (AWS), Google Cloud, or Microsoft Azure might be ideal, as they offer easy-to-use solutions for video storage, transcoding, and streaming. For larger platforms, dedicated servers or **Content Delivery**

Networks (CDNs) may be required to ensure efficient video delivery at scale.

Cloud Hosting Services

AWS (Amazon Web Services) With services like S3 for storage, EC2 for computing, and CloudFront for CDN delivery, AWS offers a powerful suite of tools for video streaming.

Google Cloud Platform Similar to AWS, Google Cloud offers tools like Cloud Storage and Compute Engine, as well as a robust CDN.

Microsoft Azure Azure provides scalable cloud services with a focus on high availability, which is critical for video streaming.

Setting Up a Streaming Server

For serving video content, you'll need a **streaming server**. The most common tools for video streaming servers are **Wowza Streaming Engine**, **Nginx with RTMP Module**, and **Flussonic Media Server**.

- **Wowza Streaming Engine** is a robust, enterprise-grade solution that supports a variety of video formats and streaming protocols.
- **Nginx with RTMP Module** is a more lightweight, open-source solution that is ideal for smaller platforms or if you're on a budget.

- **Flussonic Media Server** provides comprehensive support for live and on-demand video streaming, with advanced features like adaptive bitrate streaming.

Once you have selected your streaming server, you will need to configure it to accept incoming video files, store them, and make them available for delivery through the appropriate streaming protocol (e.g., HLS, RTMP).

Encoding and Transcoding Videos

Video encoding and transcoding are crucial steps in optimizing video files for delivery to different devices, screen sizes, and network conditions. When a user uploads a video to your platform, it must be converted into different formats and bitrates for efficient streaming. This process is called transcoding.

Understanding Video Codecs and Formats

To get started, you should have a basic understanding of the different video codecs and formats. Common video codecs include

H.264/AVC (Advanced Video Coding) The most widely used video codec for streaming video, known for balancing video quality and compression.

H.265/HEVC (High-Efficiency Video Coding) A more efficient codec that offers higher compression, allowing for better video quality at lower bitrates compared to H.264.

VP9 An open-source codec developed by Google, offering similar compression benefits to H.265.

Each video will need to be transcoded into multiple formats to ensure compatibility across various devices and browsers. For example, you might need to generate

- Low-bitrate versions for mobile networks.
- High-bitrate versions for 4K TVs.
- Adaptive bitrate versions for different internet speeds.

Setting Up Transcoding on the Server

To handle video transcoding, you can use open-source tools like **FFmpeg**, which is a powerful multimedia framework that can convert, stream, and transcode audio and video files. FFmpeg supports a wide range of codecs and formats, and it can be integrated into your platform's backend to automate the transcoding process.

FFmpeg Command Example

Alternatively, cloud services like **AWS MediaConvert**, **Google Cloud Transcoder**, or **Azure Media Services** can provide scalable and managed transcoding solutions that offload the heavy lifting to the cloud, making it easier to scale your platform.

Building a Simple Video Player

One of the most important components of any video platform is the **video player** that users interact with. Building a basic video player involves selecting a video player library and embedding it into your website or mobile app. Several libraries and tools can help you achieve this

Selecting a Video Player Library

Some of the most commonly used open-source video player libraries include

- **Video.js** A popular open-source HTML5 and Flash video player. It supports a wide range of video formats and provides a customizable player interface.
- **JW Player** A widely used commercial video player that supports adaptive streaming and a range of features for both desktop and mobile.
- **Shaka Player** An open-source JavaScript library for playing adaptive bitrate video, which supports HLS and DASH protocols.

Embedding the Video Player

To embed the video player in your platform, you will need to implement it on the frontend (typically using

149

HTML5 and JavaScript). Here's an example using **Video.js**

```
<video id="my-video" class="video-js vjs-default-skin" controls
preload="auto" width="640" height="360" data-setup="{}">
    <source src="video_file.mp4" type="video/mp4">
    <p class="vjs-no-js">To view this video, please enable
JavaScript, and consider upgrading to a web browser that
supports HTML5 video.</p>
</video>
<script src="https //vjs.zencdn.net/7.10.2/video.js"></script>
```

This basic setup will display a video player that can stream content in the specified format.

Implementing Streaming Services

Streaming services are the backbone of any video platform. To implement a reliable and scalable streaming service, you need to handle various tasks like video segmentation, delivering videos efficiently, and supporting different streaming protocols.

Adaptive Streaming with HLS/DASH

Adaptive bitrate streaming allows video players to automatically adjust the quality of the video based on the viewer's internet speed. This ensures smooth playback without buffering. The most common protocols for adaptive streaming are **HTTP Live Streaming (HLS)** and **Dynamic Adaptive Streaming over HTTP (DASH)**.

Both protocols work by breaking the video file into small chunks and serving those chunks over HTTP. The player then selects the appropriate quality level based on the user's current bandwidth.

Here's a basic example of how to implement HLS on your platform

- **Transcode videos** into HLS segments using tools like FFmpeg.
- **Host the video chunks** on your server or CDN.
- **Use the video player** (e.g., Video.js) to stream the HLS content using the .m3u8 playlist file.

Integrating with a CDN

A **Content Delivery Network (CDN)** is a network of servers distributed across various locations to deliver content more efficiently. By using a CDN, you can reduce latency and ensure that your video streams load quickly, regardless of the user's geographical location.

Popular CDNs include **Cloudflare**, **AWS CloudFront**, and **Akamai**. By integrating your video platform with a CDN, you ensure that your content is cached at various edge locations, reducing the load on your primary server and improving streaming performance.

Testing and Optimization

After setting up your video platform, it's crucial to test and optimize it for performance. Key areas to focus on include

Load testing to ensure that your servers can handle the expected traffic.

Optimizing video encoding settings to balance quality and file size.

Ensuring compatibility across devices, including desktops, smartphones, and smart TVs.

Building a video platform requires attention to detail and a well-rounded understanding of various technologies, from video encoding and streaming protocols to server setup and frontend design. By following the steps outlined in this chapter, you can create a functional video platform tailored to your needs, whether it's for personal use or as a commercial service. As you move forward, be sure to consider scalability, security, and the user experience to ensure your platform remains competitive and engaging.

Chapter 15

Troubleshooting and Optimization

In building and managing a video platform, the ability to troubleshoot issues and optimize the system for performance is critical. A video platform's success depends not only on its ability to deliver high-quality content but also on the reliability, speed, and user experience it provides. This chapter will delve into practical tips and strategies for debugging common problems, optimizing video delivery, and ensuring a seamless experience for users across various devices. The ability to identify and resolve performance bottlenecks, reduce latency, and improve video quality will give your platform the edge it needs in today's competitive market.

Identifying and Solving Performance

Performance bottlenecks in a video platform can arise at various points in the system, from video upload and encoding to playback and network delivery. A bottleneck occurs when one part of the system limits the overall performance, causing delays, buffering, or poor video quality. Understanding where and how these bottlenecks occur is the first step in solving them. Let's break down the common bottleneck areas and strategies for resolving them.

Video Encoding and Transcoding Bottlenecks

Video encoding and transcoding are resource-intensive processes that can become a significant bottleneck if not properly optimized. When a video is uploaded to the platform, it typically needs to be transcoded into multiple formats to ensure compatibility across devices and varying network conditions. This process can take a significant amount of time, especially if you are dealing with high-resolution videos like 4K content.

To address encoding bottlenecks, consider the following approaches

Use hardware acceleration Modern graphics processing units (GPUs) can significantly speed up the encoding and transcoding process compared to relying on the central processing unit (CPU) alone. Tools like **NVIDIA NVENC** and **Intel Quick Sync Video** can help accelerate the transcoding pipeline.

Optimize transcoding settings Adjust the quality and bitrate settings to find the right balance between video quality and file size. Too high a bitrate can lead to longer encoding times and larger file sizes, which can affect delivery speed.

Cloud-based transcoding services Platforms like **AWS MediaConvert**, **Google Cloud Transcoder**, and **Azure Media Services** offer scalable, cloud-based transcoding solutions that can handle large volumes of video content more efficiently than an on-premise setup.

Network and Streaming Bottlenecks

Another area where bottlenecks commonly occur is in the network delivery of video content. If your video delivery architecture is not properly optimized, users may experience buffering, lag, or low-quality video streaming, especially during peak traffic periods.

To resolve these issues

Implement a Content Delivery Network (CDN) CDNs store copies of your video content at multiple edge locations around the world, reducing the distance between the user and the content. By offloading traffic to these geographically distributed servers, CDNs reduce latency and prevent overload on your main server.

Adaptive bitrate streaming This technique allows the video player to switch between different quality levels based on the user's current network conditions. By ensuring that users receive the best quality video that their internet connection can support, you reduce the likelihood of buffering. Protocols like **HLS** and **DASH** are used to achieve adaptive bitrate streaming.

Optimize video segmentation If you are using protocols like HLS, ensure that video segments are appropriately sized. Too large segments can cause delays in starting the video, while too small segments might increase overhead.

Server Performance and Load Balancing

Server performance is another potential bottleneck, especially as your platform scales. If the server infrastructure cannot handle the increasing load of video requests, you may experience slow load times, server crashes, or issues with video delivery.

To alleviate server bottlenecks

Load balancing By distributing incoming requests across multiple servers, you can ensure that no single server bears too much load. This helps maintain system performance and availability, even during peak traffic.

Horizontal scaling Add more servers to your infrastructure to distribute the load. Using cloud services like AWS, Google Cloud, or Azure, you can scale up or down as needed to match traffic demands.

Auto-scaling Set up auto-scaling to automatically adjust your server capacity based on real-time traffic patterns. This ensures that your platform is always equipped to handle traffic spikes without manual intervention.

Reducing Latency

Latency is a critical factor in ensuring a smooth video streaming experience. High latency results in delayed video playback, causing buffering and interruptions. Reducing latency should be a priority for video platforms, especially for live streaming, where delays can be even more noticeable.

Using Low-Latency Streaming Protocols

To minimize latency in video delivery, consider switching to low-latency streaming protocols. The most common protocols for reducing latency include

Low Latency HLS (LL-HLS) A variation of the standard HLS protocol that reduces latency by segmenting videos into smaller chunks and streaming them more quickly.

WebRTC (Web Real-Time Communication) This protocol is designed specifically for low-latency, peer-to-peer communication and is ideal for real-time video applications like live streaming or video conferencing. It enables direct communication between users without requiring intermediate servers, significantly reducing latency.

RTMP (Real-Time Messaging Protocol) Though somewhat outdated, RTMP is still a widely used low-latency protocol for live streaming. It can be particularly useful for interactive streams, but newer protocols like WebRTC and LL-HLS are often more efficient.

Geographically Distributed Servers

Latency can be reduced by distributing your servers across multiple geographic regions. Using a Content Delivery Network (CDN) with edge servers in different locations helps reduce the physical distance between the video content and the end-user. This significantly lowers the time it takes for data to travel, thus improving video load times and reducing buffering.

Server Location and Infrastructure

Ensure that your primary streaming servers are located close to your user base. If you are using cloud services, take advantage of data centers that are geographically located near your target audience. If you have the option, consider utilizing **Edge Computing** at the edge of the network to handle processing closer to the user, further reducing latency.

Improving Video Quality

One of the biggest challenges for video platforms is delivering high-quality video content across a variety of devices, network conditions, and screen sizes. To ensure the best possible viewing experience, consider the following optimization strategies.

Video Compression and Bitrate Management

While high-quality video content is essential, excessive bitrate and file size can lead to slow loading times and buffer issues. Managing bitrate efficiently is essential for high-quality video delivery without overwhelming network resources.

Use efficient codecs Consider adopting the **H.265/HEVC** or **VP9** video codecs, which offer better compression and quality compared to older codecs like H.264. These codecs reduce the file size while maintaining video quality, which is crucial for streaming at high resolutions like 4K.

Dynamic bitrate adaptation By implementing adaptive bitrate streaming, your platform can automatically adjust video quality based on the user's internet speed. This ensures that users always receive the highest quality video possible without interruption.

Video Resolution and Frame Rate

Offering videos in multiple resolutions (e.g., 480p, 720p, 1080p, 4K) ensures compatibility with different devices and network conditions. For example, users on mobile devices or slower internet connections may prefer to watch at lower resolutions, while those with fast connections can enjoy high-definition content. Additionally, choosing the appropriate frame rate is crucial—standard videos typically use 24 or 30 frames per second (fps), but 60 fps can provide a smoother, higher-quality experience, especially for fast-moving content like sports.

Improving Audio and Visual Sync

Audio and visual synchronization issues can seriously affect the viewing experience. This problem can arise from network inconsistencies or issues during encoding. To mitigate this, ensure that your platform supports proper buffering techniques and keeps track of audio and video sync during encoding, playback, and delivery.

Optimizing for Cross-Device Experience

A modern video platform needs to support multiple devices and screen sizes, ranging from smartphones and tablets to smart TVs and desktop browsers. Achieving a consistent and seamless user experience across all these platforms requires thoughtful optimization strategies.

Responsive Web Design

For web-based platforms, ensure that your video player is responsive. It should automatically adjust to different screen sizes and orientations without compromising the video quality. This ensures that the video experience is as good on a desktop as it is on a mobile device or tablet.

Mobile Optimization

Optimizing video playback on mobile devices is crucial, given the growing number of mobile video consumers. Focus on reducing the amount of bandwidth needed for video delivery and ensuring smooth playback even in low-network conditions. Consider building dedicated mobile apps for iOS and Android to offer a more tailored and high-performing video experience.

Smart TV and Console Integration

When developing for Smart TVs and gaming consoles, ensure that the video player is optimized for large screens and high-definition content. The user interface should be simple and intuitive, with support for remote control navigation. Additionally, ensure that the video quality is adjusted to fit the capabilities of the television or console.

Troubleshooting and optimization are ongoing processes in the life of a video platform. As new technologies emerge and user expectations evolve, staying on top of performance issues and continuously improving video quality, reducing latency, and optimizing for different devices is essential. By understanding the common bottlenecks and applying the strategies outlined in this chapter, you can ensure that your video platform delivers a seamless, high-quality user experience that keeps users engaged and satisfied. Whether you're just starting or scaling your platform, optimization should always be a core focus to stay competitive in the fast-paced world of video streaming.

Chapter 16

Conclusion and Future Directions

As we reach the conclusion of this comprehensive exploration into the world of video platforms, it is essential to reflect on how far the industry has come and where it is heading. From the earliest days of simple video-sharing websites to the sophisticated streaming services we use today, the evolution of video platforms has been nothing short of revolutionary. The impact of this transformation is evident across multiple industries—entertainment, education, social media, marketing, and even healthcare. With the rapid advancements in technology, video platforms continue to evolve, offering more dynamic, immersive, and engaging user experiences. This chapter serves as both a reflection on the journey of video platform development and an invitation to look toward the future with curiosity, creativity, and a willingness to embrace emerging technologies.

The Evolution of Video Platforms

In the past few decades, video platforms have undergone immense changes. Early platforms like YouTube, which initially allowed users to upload and share videos with friends, have evolved into complex ecosystems capable of supporting live-streaming, virtual reality content, and even interactive features like comments, likes, and community engagement tools. The advent of high-definition (HD) and 4K video content has significantly raised the bar for quality expectations, while new innovations like 360-degree videos, augmented reality (AR), and virtual reality (VR) have made the viewing experience more immersive and interactive.

Streaming services such as Netflix, Hulu, and Amazon Prime Video have not only revolutionized how we consume television and movies but have also shifted the entire television and film industries. These platforms have fundamentally changed distribution models, replacing traditional cable and satellite services with on-demand, subscription-based services. At the same time, these platforms have fostered an explosion of content creation, democratizing media and giving rise to a diverse range of creators.

The way users engage with video has also changed drastically. Mobile devices, smart TVs, and wearable technologies now provide users with constant access to video content, irrespective of time or place. This shift in accessibility has drastically impacted the way people interact with video platforms, encouraging companies to adapt their platforms for various device types, screen sizes, and network conditions.

One of the more significant recent shifts is the integration of artificial intelligence (AI) and machine learning (ML) in video platforms. AI has made it possible for platforms to personalize content recommendations, automate subtitling and translation, and even improve video quality through enhanced encoding techniques. As machine learning continues to evolve, AI's role in video platforms will only grow, pushing forward a more personalized and intuitive viewing experience.

Looking Ahead What the Future Holds

The future of video platforms is one of immense potential. With the rapid development of new technologies, we are on the verge of new, disruptive changes that will further transform the way we experience and interact with video content.

8K Video and Beyond

While 4K video is becoming more standard, 8K video is poised to push the boundaries of video quality even further. 8K offers four times the resolution of 4K, resulting in an ultra-crisp, hyper-realistic visual experience that will be particularly transformative for entertainment, live broadcasting, and immersive content such as virtual reality (VR). However, delivering 8K content presents a significant challenge in terms of bandwidth and storage, and this will require further advances in compression algorithms and streaming technologies. The demand for 8K content will also prompt the development of higher-performance devices such as televisions, monitors, and mobile devices capable of supporting the resolution.

AI-Generated Content

Artificial intelligence is rapidly evolving, and its ability to create video content is already beginning to take shape. AI tools like Deepfake technology and automated video generation systems allow for the creation of hyper-realistic video content that is indistinguishable from reality. As AI-generated content improves, it will open up new possibilities for video platforms. Content creators will be able to generate videos more efficiently and with fewer resources, while viewers will be able to enjoy highly personalized content that feels tailor-made for them. In the future, platforms may also leverage AI to enhance video editing, automate the creation of special effects, or even develop interactive, real-time video experiences.

Virtual Reality and Augmented Reality

Both virtual reality (VR) and augmented reality (AR) technologies are already making significant strides in the world of video platforms. VR, in particular, promises to take video viewing to entirely new levels by offering fully immersive, interactive experiences. Whether it's for gaming, educational content, or immersive live events, VR will enable users to step directly into the video, giving them a new perspective and level of engagement.

AR, on the other hand, has the potential to revolutionize how we interact with the real world by overlaying digital content onto the physical environment. For video platforms, this could lead to the development of hybrid video experiences where users can engage with both digital and physical environments simultaneously. Imagine watching a live sports event through an AR lens that overlays player statistics, scoreboards, and instant replays onto the real-world view of the game.

Blockchain for Video Distribution

Blockchain technology holds the potential to significantly change the way video content is distributed, monetized, and protected. The decentralized nature of blockchain can offer transparent, secure, and tamper-proof systems for content distribution, reducing piracy and improving content creators' rights. Blockchain also opens the possibility for new, decentralized video platforms that allow creators to directly monetize their content without relying on centralized platforms like YouTube or Vimeo. Smart contracts, powered by blockchain, could enable automatic, transparent payments to creators based on user engagement, removing intermediaries and ensuring a fairer distribution of revenue.

Immersive and Interactive Video

Another exciting direction for video platforms is the evolution of interactive and immersive video. Interactive storytelling, where viewers can make decisions that influence the plot of a video, is already being explored by platforms like Netflix in shows like *Bandersnatch.* As technology improves, these experiences will become more complex and deeply integrated with VR and AR, offering users a fully immersive and customizable narrative experience. Moreover, platforms are increasingly integrating social features where viewers can interact with others in real-time while watching live video streams or pre-recorded content, creating new forms of collective viewing experiences.

Experimentation and Contribution

As the video platform landscape continues to evolve, the opportunities for innovation are boundless. For aspiring platform developers, content creators, and engineers, this is an exciting time to experiment with new technologies and contribute to the rapidly developing field. Those with the technical expertise can begin developing next-generation video experiences, leveraging cutting-edge technologies such as AI, blockchain, VR, and AR to create platforms that redefine how we experience video content.

Equally important is the role of the open-source community in driving innovation. Many of the most successful video technologies, from video compression algorithms to streaming protocols, have emerged from the open-source community. By contributing to open-source projects or developing your own tools and libraries, you can help shape the future of video platforms and make a lasting impact on the industry.

Furthermore, it is important to continue learning and staying up to date with the latest trends and advancements. The video platform space is dynamic, and by keeping pace with emerging technologies and user expectations, you will be able to build platforms that not only meet current demands but also anticipate future ones. Attending conferences, collaborating with industry peers, and engaging with online communities can help you stay ahead of the curve.

Future of Video Platforms

The journey of building, developing, and experimenting with video platforms is only just beginning. As new technologies emerge, so too will new opportunities for innovation. The future of video platforms will be shaped by advancements in resolution, interactivity, immersion, and decentralization, among others. Whether you are a content creator, a developer, or a technologist, the key to success in this space lies in continuous learning, experimentation, and a willingness to explore new possibilities. The video platform industry is dynamic, and its future will be defined by the creativity and innovation of those who dare to push the boundaries of what's possible.

As you continue your journey in the world of video platforms, remember that the field is evolving rapidly, and the next big breakthrough may be just around the corner. By staying engaged with emerging trends, contributing to the open-source community, and always being open to learning and growing, you will be well-equipped to contribute to the next generation of video experiences. The future of video platforms is limitless—embrace it with excitement, curiosity, and a willingness to innovate.

THE END